Derby Entertaining

Traditional Kentucky Recipes

McClanahan
Publishing House

International Standard Book Number 0-913383 69 4
Library of Congress Catalog Card Number 99-091763

Cover design and book layout by James Asher Graphics
Editors:
Paula Cunningham
Michelle Stone
Verne Dobbs

Special thanks to the following for recipes included in this book:
Elizabeth Ross
Curtis and Norma Grace
desha's, Lexington, Kentucky
Old Talbott Tavern, Bardstown, Kentucky

Manufactured in the United States of America

All book order correspondence should be addressed to:

McClanahan Publishing House, Inc.
P.O. Box 100
Kuttawa, KY 42055
270-388-9388
1-800-544-6959
email: kybooks@apex.net
www.kybooks.com

Introduction

Derby Entertaining, Traditional Kentucky Recipes honors America's most famous horse race, the Kentucky Derby.

Since 1875, the Run for the Roses has been held yearly on the first Saturday in May. It is run at twin-spired Churchill Downs racetrack in Louisville, drawing an international audience.

The celebration begins two weeks prior to the Derby and is filled with events from steamboat and balloon races to marathons and gala parties characterized by lavish entertaining. Throughout the Bluegrass state, Kentuckians open their homes to guests for fun-filled socials which center around the finest dishes from Kentucky.

The race-day activities usually include a traditional Derby Day Breakfast followed by the race itself at 5 p.m. Television game-watching parties have become popular for those who are less inspired by race crowds.

The foods synonymous with this historic sports event are often prepared from traditional recipes, handed down by perennial hostesses, as well as modern dishes requiring less preparation time. Whichever version is served, one thing is certain— Derby guests are in for gastronomic treats with wonderful memories.

Derby Entertaining presents recipes you and your guests will enjoy. *Derby Entertaining* presents the foods all will remember.

Table of Contents

Appetizers
&
Beverages

Beer Cheese

Two 10-ounce packages Cracker Barrel extra sharp Cheddar cheese, grated
2 minced garlic cloves
1/2 medium onion, minced
1/4 teaspoon cayenne pepper
1/4 teaspoon Tabasco sauce
1/8 teaspoon salt
7-ounce bottle stale beer

Combine all ingredients in mixing bowl; mix thoroughly. The mixture will be soft but will harden when chilled. Chill for at least 24 hours before serving. Remove from refrigerator 30 minutes before serving and beat again.

Benedictine Cheese Spread

1 medium cucumber, peeled and seeded
8-ounce package cream cheese, softened
1 small onion, finely ground
1/2 teaspoon salt
Dash of Tabasco sauce
Mayonnaise
2 drops green food coloring

Finely grind cucumber pulp. Place in a piece of cheesecloth and press out juice until pulp is fairly dry. In a mixing bowl mash cheese with a fork. Work cucumber pulp into cheese; add onion, salt and Tabasco sauce. Add enough mayonnaise to make a smooth, easy to spread filling. Add just enough food coloring to make cheese a pale green. Mix thoroughly and use to make finger sandwiches or use as stuffing for celery.

Triple Crown Brie Appetizer

3/4 cup finely chopped and roasted pecans
1/4 cup coffee-flavored liqueur
3 tablespoons brown sugar
14-ounce mini Brie
Apples and/or pears

Remove rind from top of Brie; discard rind. Add liqueur and sugar to pecans; stir well. Place Brie on a microwave-safe serving plate. Spoon pecan mixture over top of Brie. Microwave uncovered at High for 1 1/2 to 2 minutes or until Brie softens to desired consistency, giving dish a half-turn after 1 minute. Serve with fresh diced apples and/or pears that have been dipped in fruit juice to prevent turning brown.

Derby Spread

1 pound softened butter
1 pound softened bleu cheese
1/2 cup bourbon

Cream butter and cheese together. Add bourbon slowly, mixing well. Shape into a ball and chill for 24 hours. Serve with crackers.

Bluegrass Cheese Ball

2 pounds Old English cheese
5-ounce jar bleu cheese spread
8-ounce package cream cheese
Chopped walnuts or pecans

Bring cheeses to room temperature. Mix well in large bowl of electric mixer. Cover; refrigerate for 1 hour. Roll into 3 or 4 large balls. Roll each ball in walnuts or pecans. Refrigerate or freeze until a few hours before serving. Serve at room temperature with crackers.

Olive-Nut Cheese Spread

1/2 to 3/4 cup ripe or stuffed olives, chopped
1/2 to 3/4 cup chopped pecans
8-ounce package cream cheese, softened
Mayonnaise

Mix together olives, nuts and cheese. Add enough mayonnaise to make a smooth spreading consistency. Salt and small amount of prepared horseradish may be added to give a more tangy taste. This spread may be made without cheese to make a sandwich filling.

Cheese Pecan Wafers

1 cup butter, softened
2 cups flour
1/2 pound sharp Cheddar cheese, grated
1 beaten egg
Pecan halves
Salt

Using your hands mix butter, flour and cheese. Roll out thinly between 2 sheets waxed paper. Cut out rounds with 1-1/2 inch biscuit cutter. Place on baking sheet; brush with beaten egg. Place pecan half on top of each wafer. Bake at 350° for 10 minutes. As soon as you remove them from the oven, sprinkle lightly with salt. Makes about 70 wafers.

Derby Afternoon Cheese Straws

1/2 pound grated extra sharp Cheddar cheese
1/4 pound softened butter
1/2 teaspoon salt
1/8 teaspoon cayenne pepper
1 1/2 cups flour

Combine all ingredients into a dough that is soft and pliable. You may want to add a few drops of water. Roll out dough on a lightly floured board. Cut into strips with a sharp knife or pizza cutter. Place on a shiny ungreased baking sheet. Bake at 325° for 20 minutes until straws begin to brown very lightly around the edges. Let cool on baking sheet. If desired, sprinkle lightly with paprika and salt. Store in airtight container between sheets of waxed paper. Makes 6 dozen straws.

Kentucky Vegetable Dip

8-ounce package softened cream cheese
4 ounces softened bleu cheese
1/3 cup mayonnaise
3 drops Worcestershire sauce
1 tablespoon dried onion flakes
2 drops Tabasco sauce

In a mixing bowl combine cream cheese, bleu cheese and mayonnaise. Mix well; add remaining ingredients. Beat with electric mixer until dip is smooth, adding more mayonnaise if necessary to thin. Chill; serve with raw vegetables.

Artichoke Dip

Two 15-ounce cans artichoke hearts, drained
2 cups freshly grated Parmesan cheese
1 1/2 cups mayonnaise
Butter flavored crackers

Chop artichoke hearts and put in a mixing bowl. Add Parmesan cheese and mayonnaise. Blend well. Transfer to an ovenproof serving dish. Bake at 350° for 15-20 minutes until golden and bubbly. Serve with butter flavored crackers.

Asparagus Rolls

1 loaf white sandwich bread
1 egg
8-ounce package softened cream cheese
4-ounce package softened bleu cheese
2 pounds asparagus,
trimmed and cooked in boiling water until crisp-tender
2 sticks butter, melted

Trim crusts from bread slices and roll each thin with a rolling pin. Beat egg; mix with cheeses. Spread cheese mixture on each bread slice. Roll 1 stalk of asparagus in each slice of bread; dip into melted butter. Place seam side down on a baking sheet. Freeze for 1 hour. When ready to bake, defrost slightly; cut each roll into 3 pieces. Bake at 400° for 15 minutes until rolls start to brown. Makes about 24 rolls.

Cucumber Sandwiches

2 medium-size cucumbers
2 teaspoons salt
Bottled mayonnaise with horseradish
or 1 tablespoon horseradish mixed into 1 cup mayonnaise

Pare and slice cucumber very fine. Taste raw cucumber to see if it's bitter. Once in a while one does get a bitter cucumber and it's best to buy an extra one just in case this should happen. Sprinkle with 2 teaspoons salt and let stand for several hours in refrigerator. Drain water. Use very thin white bread, or cut regular slice in half horizontally. Spread with thin layer of horseradish-mayonnaise and cucumbers. Cover with bread and gently press together. Trim edge of bread and cut in half. Keep cool until serving. Makes 40 sandwiches.

Baby Hot Browns

1 chicken bouillon cube
1/4 cup hot water
3/4 cup half and half
3 tablespoons butter
2 tablespoons flour
1 cup grated Swiss cheese
5 slices bacon, cooked, drained and crumbled
1 onion, thinly sliced
6 ounces cooked turkey, thinly sliced
18 slices party rye bread
Parsley

Dissolve bouillon cube in hot water and add half and half. Set aside. Melt butter and add flour; whisk until frothy. Add bouillon mixture and cook, stirring constantly, until bubbly and thickened. Add cheese and stir until smooth. Put bread slices in shallow baking pan. Place turkey and onion on each bread slice. Top with sauce and bacon. Bake at 350° for 10 minutes. Garnish with parsley. Makes 18 servings.

Country Ham Balls

4 cups ground cooked country ham
1 cup dried bread crumbs
2 eggs
1/2 cup milk
1/2 cup vinegar
1/2 cup water
1 cup brown sugar
2 teaspoons prepared mustard

Combine ham, bread crumbs, eggs and milk in bowl. Form into small meatballs. Place in shallow baking dish. In another bowl mix together vinegar, water, brown sugar and mustard. Pour over meatballs. Bake at 350° until brown, about 25 minutes.

Country Ham Biscuit Filling

1 cup ground cooked country ham
4 tablespoons butter

Combine ham and butter in small bowl. Split hot bite-size biscuits in half. Use about 1 tablespoon filling for each biscuit. Makes enough filling for 36 biscuits.

Hall of Fame
Country Ham Cups

2 cups finely ground, cooked country ham
1 cup finely grated sharp Cheddar cheese
Mayonnaise
24 very thin slices fresh white bread

In bowl combine ham and cheese. Add just enough mayonnaise to bind all together. Cut a circle from each slice of bread using a biscuit cutter. Place between 2 sheets waxed paper and flatten with rolling pin. Butter cups of miniature muffin tins. Press a round of bread into each cup. Bake at 375° until lightly browned, about 10 minutes. Fill each cup with ham mixture; bake at 325° until cheese is melted, about 15 minutes. Serve hot. Makes 24.

Country Ham Mousse

2 tablespoons unflavored gelatin
1/2 cup cold water
1 cup whipping cream
4 tablespoons mayonnaise
2 cups ground, cooked country ham
2 teaspoons prepared mustard
1 teaspoon prepared horseradish
Canola oil

Dissolve gelatin in cold water. Whip cream; add mayonnaise. Strain gelatin into cream mixture. Combine ham, mustard and horseradish. Add ham mixture to cream. Brush one-quart mold with canola oil and invert it on a paper towel to drain off excess oil. Pour mousse into mold, smooth with a spatula. Chill for 2 hours until firm. Unmold onto chilled platter. Serve immediately or refrigerate for 3 to 4 hours. Makes 6 servings.

Sausage Empanadas

1/2 pound bulk Italian sausage
14.5-ounce can pizza sauce
10-ounce can refrigerated flaky biscuits
4 ounces mozzarella cheese cut into 1/4 inch cubes
1 beaten egg

Brown sausage; drain. Stir in 3 tablespoons of the pizza sauce. Heat oven to 375°. Separate dough into 10 biscuits; divide each in half horizontally, forming 20 rounds. Press each round into 4-inch circle. Place 1 tablespoon meat mixture in center of each circle. Top each with cheese; press lightly. Fold dough over filling to form half circle, stretching to fit. Press edges together; seal and prick with fork. Place on ungreased cookie sheet; brush with egg. Bake for 9 to 14 minutes or until golden. Heat remaining pizza sauce and use for dipping. Makes 20.

Mini-Reubens

1/4 cup Thousand Island salad dressing
24 slices snack rye bread
1/2 pound thinly sliced corned beef
1 1/2 cups chopped sauerkraut, well drained
4 ounces sliced Swiss cheese

Heat oven to 400°. Spread about 1/2 teaspoon salad dressing on each slice of bread; place on ungreased cookie sheet. Top each with slice of corned beef and about 1 tablespoon sauerkraut. Cut cheese to fit bread; place on top. Bake for 10 minutes or until cheese is melted. Makes 24.

Finish Line Snack Squares

Two 8-ounce cans refrigerated crescent dinner rolls
6-ounce can refried beans
1 cup dairy sour cream
2 tablespoons dry taco seasoning mix
1 1/2 cups shredded Cheddar cheese
1/2 cup sliced green onions
1/2 cup chopped green pepper
1 cup chopped seeded tomatoes
1/2 cup sliced ripe olives

Unroll dough into 4 long rectangles. Place crosswise in ungreased 15x10x1-inch baking pan; press over bottom and 1-inch up sides to form crust. Firmly press perforations to seal. Bake at 375° for 15 minutes or until golden brown. Cool completely. Spread beans over crust to within 1/2-inch of edges. Combine sour cream and taco seasoning mix. Spread over beans. Sprinkle cheese, onions, green pepper, tomatoes and olives evenly over sour cream mixture. Cover; refrigerate 1 hour. Cut into squares. Makes 48.

Bourbon Pate

1/2 pound butter
1 small onion, coarsely chopped
1 pound chicken livers
1 1/2 cups chicken broth, divided
3 tablespoons sweet sherry
1/2 teaspoon paprika
1/4 teaspoon allspice
1/2 teaspoon salt
1/8 teaspoon white pepper
1 garlic clove, minced
1/2 cup bourbon
1 envelope unflavored gelatin
1 cup chopped walnuts

Melt butter in skillet. Add onion and chicken livers; cook 10 minutes, stirring occasionally. Add 3/4 cup broth, sherry, paprika, allspice, salt, pepper and garlic. Cook for 5 minutes, stirring occasionally. Remove from heat; add bourbon. Soften gelatin in remaining 3/4 cup broth. Cook over boiling water until dissolved. Transfer chicken liver mixture to blender. Process until smooth. Stir gelatin and walnuts into chicken liver mixture. Spoon into 6-cup mold and chill until firm.

Crab Triangles

6 English muffins
7-ounce can crab meat, drained
8 tablespoons margarine
7-ounce jar sharp Cheddar cheese
2 tablespoons margarine
1/2 teaspoon seasoned salt
1/2 teaspoon garlic salt

Slice muffins in half and cut each half into fourths. Combine remaining ingredients. Spread mixture on triangles. Freeze at least 30 minutes. Broil until puffed, bubbly and slightly browned. Makes 48.

Mushroom & Cheese Canapés

1/4 pound mushrooms, sliced in tiny pieces
1 tablespoon butter
8-ounce package cream cheese
1 tablespoon minced onion
1 tablespoon milk
Salt and pepper to taste
30 slices pumpernickel cocktail bread
Butter, softened

Cook mushrooms in butter. Mix with next four ingredients. Toast slices of bread in broiler until hot. Turn over and spread with butter and mushroom mixture. Place under broiler until puffy and brown. Makes 30.

Spring Morning Mimosas

4 cups club soda, chilled
12-ounce can frozen orange juice concentrate
2 bottles champagne, chilled

Blend 1 cup club soda and orange juice concentrate in blender. Pour into a punch bowl; stir in remaining club soda. Slowly add champagne. Float orange slices if desired. Serves 20.

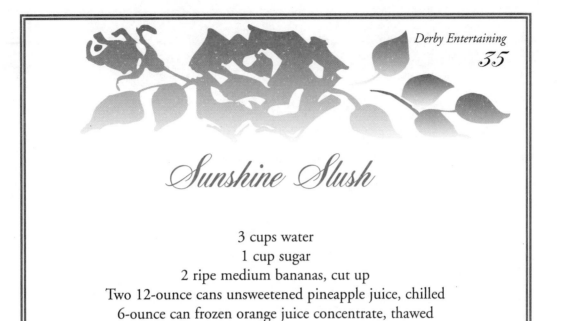

Sunshine Slush

3 cups water
1 cup sugar
2 ripe medium bananas, cut up
Two 12-ounce cans unsweetened pineapple juice, chilled
6-ounce can frozen orange juice concentrate, thawed
6-ounce can frozen lemonade concentrate, thawed
2 tablespoons lemon juice
1 1/2 cups rum or vodka
28-ounce bottle club soda, chilled

In saucepan combine water and sugar; bring to a boil stirring until sugar is dissolved. Boil gently for 3 minutes; remove from heat and cool. Meanwhile combine bananas and half the pineapple juice in a blender container. Cover and blend until smooth. Stir into cooled syrup. Stir in the remaining pineapple juice, orange and lemonade concentrates and lemon juice. Stir in rum or vodka. Turn into 13x9x2-inch pan or plastic freezer container. Cover and freeze for several hours. When ready to serve, remove from freezer and let stand at room temperature 5 to 10 minutes. Draw a large spoon across surface of frozen mixture to make slush; scoop into punch bowl. Slowly pour in club soda down side of bowl. Stir gently to combine. Makes about 14 cups punch.

Bloody Mary Pitcher

1 cup vodka
4 cups tomato juice
4 teaspoons lemon juice
4 teaspoons Worcestershire sauce
2 dashes hot pepper sauce
1 teaspoon celery salt
1 teaspoon salt
Pinch of garlic salt
Celery sticks for garnish

Mix all ingredients except celery sticks in blender. Pour into a pitcher filled with cracked ice. Serve in tall glasses with celery sticks. Makes 6 servings.

For Clam Tomato Cocktails, substitute chilled tomato-clam juice for the tomato juice.

Day's End Coffee Punch

4 quarts strong coffee
1 quart whipping cream
3 tablespoons sugar
5 teaspoons vanilla extract
2 quarts vanilla ice cream

Brew coffee and chill in refrigerator. When ready to serve, whip cream, adding sugar and vanilla. Spoon ice cream into a punch bowl. Add whipped cream and pour chilled coffee over all. Makes 50 servings.

Mock Mint Julep

4 mint sprigs
1 1/2 cups sugar
2 cups cold water
3/4 cup fresh lemon juice
1 1/2 quarts ginger ale
Thin lemon slices

Rinse mint and discard stems. Place sugar, water and lemon juice in medium-sized bowl. Mix; stir in mint leaves. Allow to stand for 30 minutes. Fill a large pitcher with ice cubes; stir liquid over ice. Add ginger ale and lemon slices. Pour into tall glasses. Serves 10.

Strawberry-Lemonade Punch

Two 6-ounce cans frozen pink lemonade concentrate, undiluted
6-ounce can frozen orange juice concentrate, undiluted
10-ounce package frozen sliced strawberries
3 cups water
28-ounce bottle ginger ale, chilled

In punch bowl, combine pink lemonade, orange juice, strawberries and water.
Refrigerate. To serve, pour ginger ale into juice mixture in bowl. Stir well.
Makes 2 1/2 quarts.

Plantation Tea

4 tea bags
1 1/2 cups sugar
1/2 cup lemon juice
4 cups boiling water
4 cups cold water
1 teaspoon almond extract
1 teaspoon vanilla

Place tea bags, sugar and lemon juice in a large metal bowl. Pour boiling water over. Cover; let steep about 15 minutes. Pour remaining ingredients in a large pitcher. Add ice and tea mixture. Stir to combine. Garnish with lemon slices if desired. Serves 8.

Breads

Beaten Biscuits

3 cups flour
1 teaspoon sugar
1/2 teaspoon salt
1/2 teaspoon baking powder
1/3 cup solid shortening
1/4 cup ice water
1/4 cup milk

In a food processor fitted with chopping blade, combine flour, sugar, salt and baking powder. Add shortening and process just until mixture resembles coarse cornmeal. With processor running, add water and then milk, a little at a time. Process for 5 minutes until dough looks crumbly. Turn dough out onto a lightly floured board; knead to form a ball. Cut dough into 18 pieces and roll each into a ball. Press down to flatten. Place biscuits 1-inch apart on a lightly greased baking sheet. Pierce tops 3 times with a fork. Bake in pre-heated 400° oven for 25 minutes or until they start to brown. Makes 18 biscuits.

Derby Breakfast Yeast Biscuits

1 package instant dry yeast
1 cup warm buttermilk
1/2 teaspoon baking soda
1 teaspoon salt
2 tablespoons sugar
2 1/2 cups flour
1/2 cup solid shortening
Melted butter

Dissolve yeast in buttermilk and set aside. Sift baking soda, salt, sugar and flour into bowl. Cut in shortening with pastry blender until mixture resembles coarse cornmeal. Add yeast mixture; stir until just blended. Knead gently. Roll out on lightly floured board to 1/2-inch thickness. Cut with 2-inch biscuit cutter and dip in butter. Place 1-inch apart on lightly greased baking sheet. Let rise for 1 hour. Bake at 400° for 12 minutes. Makes 18 biscuits. May be used for ham and biscuits. When done fill with thinly-sliced cooked country ham.

Out of the Gate Ham Biscuits

1 cup flour
2 teaspoons baking powder
1/8 teaspoon salt
1/4 teaspoon dry mustard
3 tablespoons solid shortening
1 cup cooked ground country ham
1/2 cup or less milk

Combine flour, baking powder, salt and mustard in bowl. Using a pastry blender cut in shortening until mixture resembles coarse cornmeal. Add ham and enough milk to make a soft dough. Turn out onto lightly floured board; knead for 30 seconds. Roll out to 3/4-inch thickness. Cut with small biscuit cutter. Place on lightly greased baking sheet. Bake in preheated 450° oven for 10 minutes. Serve with butter. Makes 24 biscuits.

Beer Biscuits

3 cups biscuit mix
3 tablespoons sugar
12-ounce can beer

Mix dry ingredients first. Pour in beer and stir until blended. It does not need to be smooth. Fill greased muffin tins half full. Bake at 400° for 15 minutes. Serves 8.

Fabulous French Bread

Two 8-ounce packages Swiss cheese slices
2 loaves French bread, sliced lengthwise
1 cup butter
2 tablespoons poppy seeds
2 tablespoons prepared mustard
1/4 cup chopped onion
4 strips bacon

Place slices of Swiss cheese between sliced loaves of bread. Mix butter, poppy seed, and mustard; cook over low heat. Sprinkle onion over bread and pour butter mixture over it. Put 2 strips bacon on top of each loaf. Wrap each loaf in foil with the seam side up. Bake at 400° for 20 minutes. Broil one minute to crisp bacon. Makes 12 servings.

Lemon Bread

1/3 cup solid shortening
1 1/3 cups sugar, divided
2 eggs
1 1/2 cups sifted flour
1 1/2 teaspoon baking powder
1/4 teaspoon salt
1/2 cup milk
Grated rind of 1 lemon
1/2 cup chopped pecans
Juice of 1 lemon

Cream shortening and sugar in large bowl of electric mixer until light and fluffy. Beat in eggs, one at a time. Beat in dry ingredients alternately with milk. Stir in rind and nuts. Spoon into large greased loaf pan. Bake at 350° for 1 hour. Mix juice and remaining sugar. Pour over hot bread and cool. Makes 1 loaf.

Cherry Banana Bread

1/2 cup dried cherries
1/2 cup flour
1/2 teaspoon baking powder
1/4 teaspoon baking soda
1 teaspoon cinnamon
3/4 cup whole-wheat flour
2 tablespoons cornmeal
1 ripe banana, chopped
1/2 cup brown sugar
1 egg
1 tablespoon oil
3/4 cup buttermilk
1 tablespoon grated orange zest

Soak cherries in warm water for 30 minutes. Sift together flour, baking powder, baking soda, and cinnamon in a large bowl. Add whole-wheat flour and cornmeal; stir to blend. In a blender, combine banana, brown sugar, egg, oil, buttermilk, and orange zest. Stir blended ingredients into dry ingredients; gently stir until completely mixed. Drain cherries and add to batter. Spoon into a lightly greased loaf pan and bake at 350° for 40 minutes. Makes 1 loaf.

Poppy Cheese Bread

2 1/2 cups biscuit mix
2 cups shredded sharp Cheddar cheese
2 teaspoons poppy seeds
1 teaspoon garlic powder
2 eggs
1 cup milk
1 stick margarine, melted

Combine biscuit mix, cheese, poppy seeds, and garlic powder. Combine eggs, milk and margarine; add to biscuit mixture. Stir vigorously until well blended. Spoon into a lightly greased loaf pan and bake at 350° for 35 minutes. Makes 1 loaf.

Raisin Bread

3 1/2 cups flour
1 teaspoon salt
4 teaspoons baking powder
1/4 teaspoon cinnamon
2 eggs
4 tablespoons melted butter
4 tablespoons sugar
1 cup milk
1 1/2 cups chopped raisins

Sift together flour, salt, baking powder and cinnamon in mixing bowl. In another bowl, beat eggs; add butter, sugar and milk. Combine with dry ingredients. Stir in raisins until well mixed. Spoon into greased loaf pan; let stand for 10 minutes. Bake in 350° oven for 45 minutes. Makes 1 loaf.

Sally Lunn Bread

1/2 cup butter
1 tablespoon sugar
1/2 teaspoon salt
2 beaten eggs
1 cup milk
1 cake of yeast
3 cups flour

Cream together butter, sugar and salt. Add eggs and beat well. Heat milk to lukewarm. Add yeast to milk to dissolve. Add to butter and egg mixture. Stir in flour, mixing well. Spoon into buttered tube pan. Let rise for 1 1/2 hours or until double in bulk. Bake at 350° for 50 minutes. Serve hot with butter. Makes 1 loaf.

Bourbon Bread

3/4 cup raisins
1/3 cup bourbon
1 1/4 cups softened butter
1 1/2 cups sugar
6 eggs, separated
2 1/4 cups flour
1 1/4 teaspoons vanilla extract
1 cup coarsely broken pecans

Soak raisins in bourbon for 2 hours. Drain, reserving bourbon. Add more bourbon to make 1/3 cup. Cream butter and 1/2 cup sugar until light and fluffy. Add egg yolks one at a time, beating well. Add flour in thirds, alternately with bourbon; mix until well blended. Stir in raisins, vanilla and pecans. Beat egg whites until soft peaks form. Gradually add remaining cup of sugar; beat until stiff. Gently fold into bread batter. Line bottoms of 2 loaf pans with greased waxed paper. Spoon in batter. Bake at 350° for 1 hour. Makes 2 loaves.

Bourbon Sticky Buns

1 package hot roll mix
1/4 cup scalded milk, cooled to lukewarm
1 egg
1/2 cup bourbon
2 3/4 cups brown sugar
1 cup pecan halves
1/4 cup softened butter
2 teaspoons cinnamon

Make dough according to package directions, except use milk instead of water and add the egg. Grease 18 muffin cups. Into each cup measure 3/4 teaspoon bourbon, 1 1/2 teaspoons brown sugar and 3 or 4 pecans. Roll dough on a lightly floured board into a 12x18" rectangle. Combine remaining bourbon, brown sugar, butter and cinnamon and spread on dough. Roll up jelly-roll fashion, beginning at the narrow end. Cut roll into 18 slices. Place a slice in each muffin cup. Cover pans and let rise for 30 minutes. Bake at 375° for 20 minutes until nicely browned. Cool on wire racks for 5 minutes before turning buns out of pans. Best served warm. Makes 18 buns.

Cheesy Yeast Rolls

1 package dry yeast
1/4 cup warm water
1/3 cup milk
1/2 cup softened butter
1 egg
2 tablespoons sugar
1/2 teaspoon salt
2 1/2 cups flour
2 tablespoons chopped green pepper
1 tablespoon chopped pimiento
1/3 cup finely grated Cheddar cheese

Dissolve yeast in warm water. In large bowl of electric mixer combine milk, butter, egg, sugar and salt at low speed. Add 1 1/2 cups flour. Mix in dissolved yeast and beat 1 minute at medium speed. Add green pepper, pimiento and remaining flour. Stir in cheese. Spoon into greased muffin cups, cover and let rise for 1 hour. Bake at 400° for 20 minutes until golden brown. Makes 24 rolls.

High Stakes Nutty Bread Cups

2 cups Bisquick
1/2 cup sugar
1/4 cup flour
1 egg
3/4 cup milk
1 cup finely chopped nuts

Combine all ingredients in mixing bowl. Grease and flour small muffin pans. Fill 2/3 full; bake at 350° for about 20 minutes until golden brown. When cool, scoop out the middle of muffin. Butter and fill with chicken salad. Makes 18 cups.

Corn Spoonbread

2 cups milk
3/4 cup cornmeal
1 tablespoon sugar
1/2 teaspoon baking powder
1/4 teaspoon salt
Pepper to taste
4 eggs, separated
1 cup frozen corn kernels, thawed
Vegetable oil for baking dish

Preheat oven to 350°. In a saucepan, scald milk to near boiling; gradually stir in cornmeal. Stir until very thick, about 2 minutes. Remove from heat; stir in sugar, baking powder and salt. Sprinkle with pepper. Add egg yolks and corn; blend well. In another bowl, whip egg whites until stiff. Fold into cornmeal mixture. Spoon batter into an oiled 1 1/2 quart soufflé dish; bake for 40 minutes. Makes 6 servings.

deSha's Fabulous Cornbread

2 cups self-rising cornmeal
6 eggs
20 ounces cream style corn
3 cups sour cream
1 1/2 cups salad oil
1/3 cup sugar

Combine all ingredients, mixing well. Pour into well-greased 15x10x2-inch pan. Bake at 350° for about 40 minutes, or until a pick comes out clean.

Eggs Derby

6 hard-cooked eggs
3/4 cup cooked country ham, minced
3 tablespoons heavy cream
Salt and pepper to taste
4 tablespoons butter, divided
2 tablespoons flour
1 1/2 cups scalded milk
1 1/2 cups scalded heavy cream
6 large mushrooms, sliced
1/4 cup butter
1/4 cup grated Parmesan cheese
1/2 teaspoon paprika

Remove shells and carefully cut eggs in half lengthwise. Remove yolks and mix with ham, cream, salt and pepper. Fill egg white halves with yolk mixture. Place in buttered 9x9x2-inch baking dish. In saucepan, melt 2 tablespoons butter; stir in flour until smooth. Remove from heat. Add scalded milk and scalded cream. Stir until smooth; add more salt and pepper to taste. Simmer for 10 minutes. In skillet, sauté mushrooms in 1/4 cup butter. Season with salt and pepper and add to cream sauce. Pour over eggs. Sprinkle with Parmesan cheese and top with 2 tablespoons butter and paprika. Bake at 450° for 10 minutes until golden. Makes 6 servings.

Egg and Mushroom Casserole

3/4 cup butter, divided
1 pound sliced fresh mushrooms
10 hard-cooked eggs, chopped
2 tablespoons flour
2 cups whipping cream
Pepper, Cayenne and Salt to taste
1 cup breadcrumbs
1 cup shredded Cheddar cheese
Cooked bacon pieces

Melt 1/4 cup butter over low heat. Add mushrooms; cook until tender. Combine mushrooms and eggs in mixing bowl. Spoon into lightly-greased casserole dish and set aside. Melt 1/4 cup of butter in top of double-boiler over hot water. Add flour, blending well. Gradually add cream, stirring constantly. Cook until thickened. Remove from heat; season with pepper, cayenne pepper and salt. Pour sauce over mushrooms and egg mixture. Melt remaining 1/4 cup of butter in skillet over low heat. Add breadcrumbs and cheese, stirring to combine. Pour over sauce mixture. Sprinkle with bacon pieces. Bake at 375° for 20 minutes until top is well browned. Makes 6 servings.

Brunch Eggs

3 dozen eggs
1/4 cup milk
1/4 pound butter, melted
3 cans mushroom soup
1/2 cup sherry
1 large can mushrooms, drained
4 cups cubed, cooked ham
1/2 pound grated Cheddar cheese
Paprika

Combine eggs and milk in mixing bowl. Scramble egg mixture in melted butter. In saucepan heat soup, sherry and mushrooms. In large buttered baking dish layer egg mixture, soup mixture and ham. Sprinkle with cheese and paprika. Bake at 250° for 1 hour. Makes 18 servings.

Derby Day Cheese Soufflé

3 tablespoons butter
3 tablespoons flour
1 cup scalded milk
1/2 cup grated sharp Cheddar cheese
1 teaspoon salt
4 eggs, divided
1 additional egg white

In double-boiler over hot water melt butter and blend in flour. Gradually stir in milk, blending until smooth and thick. Add cheese and salt. Beat the egg yolks until light and lemon colored and pour the cream mixture into eggs. Beat egg whites until stiff but still moist. Fold half of egg whites into cream sauce fairly well. Fold second half in just lightly. Pour mixture into greased soufflé dish or straight-sided casserole. Bake uncovered in 375° oven until soufflé has puffed up and browned, about 35 minutes. Serve at once or it will fall. Serves 4.

Cheese Grits Casserole

2 cups instant grits
3 cups boiling water
1 stick butter
6-ounce tube garlic cheese spread
1 teaspoon salt
2 well-beaten eggs

Stir grits into boiling water. Remove from heat; add butter, cheese, salt and eggs. Pour into well-buttered casserole dish. Bake at 350° for 45 minutes until set and light brown on top. Makes 8 servings.

Country Ham Puff

4 slices white bread, torn
2 cups milk
3 eggs
1/2 teaspoon spicy mustard
1/8 teaspoon paprika
Dash of garlic powder
2 cups shredded Cheddar cheese
1 1/2 cups diced cooked country ham
1/2 cup chopped onion
4 slices bacon, cooked, drained and crumbled
2 tablespoons chopped fresh parsley

Combine bread, milk, eggs, mustard, paprika and garlic powder in bowl. Beat at medium speed of electric mixer until smooth, about 1 minute. Stir in cheese, ham, onion, bacon and parsley. Spoon into greased 12x8x2-inch baking dish. Bake at 375° for 30 minutes. Let stand 10 minutes before serving. Makes 8 servings.

Sautéed Sausage and Grits

1 cup quick grits
4 cups chicken broth
1/2 cup cornmeal
1 pound bulk sausage, fried and drained
3 beaten eggs
Salt, pepper and cayenne pepper to taste
Canola oil

Cook grits in boiling chicken broth until thick. Add cornmeal, sausage, eggs, salt, pepper and cayenne pepper. Spoon into a loaf pan and chill overnight. Unmold, cut into 1/2-inch slices and sauté in oil until crusty and browned. Serve with maple syrup. Makes 16 servings.

Fast Break Sausage and Egg Casserole

1 1/2 pounds bulk sausage
9 lightly beaten eggs
3 cups milk
1 1/2 teaspoons dry mustard
1 teaspoon salt
3 slices white bread, cut into 1/8-inch cubes
1 1/2 cups grated Cheddar cheese

Brown sausage and drain. Spread into greased 13x9x2-inch pan. In mixing bowl, combine eggs, milk, dry mustard, salt, bread cubes and cheese. Spread over sausage. Cover and chill overnight. Uncover and bake at 350° for 1 hour. Cut into squares to serve. Makes 8 servings.

Creole Eggs Curtis Lee

1 medium-size onion, finely chopped
2 tablespoons bacon fat
15-ounce can tomatoes
Salt and pepper to taste
Dash of Tabasco sauce
1/2 cup butter, divided
3 heaping tablespoons flour
1 cup milk
8 large hard-boiled eggs
1 cup toasted bread crumbs

Sauté onions in bacon fat. Add tomatoes; simmer until onions are well done. Add salt, Tabasco and pepper to taste. This mixture should be highly seasoned. Make a white sauce of 1/4 cup butter, all the flour and milk. Sauce should be thick. Add tomato mixture to white sauce; stir well. Slice eggs into well buttered casserole; pour tomato mixture over eggs. Mix bread crumbs with remaining butter; sprinkle on top. Bake at 325° until crumbs are brown. Chopped bell peppers may be added with onions if you like. Serves 6 to 8.

Norma's Bacon

Medium to thick sliced bacon
Milk
Plain or self-rising flour

Dip bacon slices into milk then into flour. Place on cookie sheet sprayed with nonstick spray. Bake at 325° until brown and crispy. Drain on paper towels.

Eggs Benedict

4 English muffins, split
Butter or margarine
8 slices boneless cooked ham, broiled
8 eggs, poached

Hollandaise Sauce:

1 cup butter or margarine
4 eggs
2 tablespoons lemon juice
1/4 teaspoon cayenne pepper
1/2 teaspoon salt
1/2 cup hot water

Prepare Hollandaise Sauce: Melt butter in top of double boiler. Beat eggs until blended and gradually pour the hot butter over the eggs, beating constantly with a wire whip. Return butter-egg mixture to top of double boiler. Stir over hot water until thickened. Add lemon juice, cayenne, pepper, salt and hot water; stir until blended. Keep warm while making eggs. Makes 2 cups sauce.

Toast and butter muffin halves; keep them warm. To serve, place a slice of ham on each muffin half, top with poached egg and cover with warm Hollandaise. Sprinkle with paprika and garnish with parsley. Serves 8.

Pineapple Brunch Casserole

8-ounce can crushed pineapple
1 cup Bisquick mix
1 cup milk
4 slightly beaten eggs
6 tablespoons melted butter or margarine
1 teaspoon Dijon mustard
1/2 teaspoon onion powder
Pinch of ground nutmeg
4 ounces cooked ham, diced
1 cup shredded Monterey Jack cheese
2 finely chopped green onions

Drain pineapple; reserve 2 tablespoons for garnish. Beat Bisquick mix, milk, eggs, butter, mustard, onion powder and nutmeg in large mixer bowl until smooth. Stir in ham, cheese, onions and pineapple. Pour into greased 9-inch pie plate. Bake at 350° for 35 to 40 minutes or until set. Garnish with reserved pineapple. Serves 6.

Breakfast Fruit Salad

1 cup sour cream
2 tablespoons honey
2 tablespoons orange juice
4 bananas, sliced
2 oranges, pared and sectioned
2 cups strawberries, cut in half
1 1/2 cups granola

Mix sour cream, honey and orange juice. Arrange fruit in glass bowl. Top with sour cream mixture and granola. Serves 8.

And They're Off French Toast

Margarine
1 long thin loaf Italian bread
8 large eggs
3 cups milk
4 teaspoons sugar
1/2 teaspoon cinnamon
1 tablespoon vanilla
2 tablespoons butter or margarine, cut into pieces

Grease one 9x13-inch baking dish with margarine. Cut bread into inch-thick slices and arrange in one layer on bottom of dish. Beat eggs with remaining ingredients, except butter. Pour over bread slices. Cover with foil and refrigerate overnight. Dot bread with butter or margarine pieces. Bake at 350° for 50 minutes until bread is puffy and lightly browned. Let stand about 5 minutes before serving.

Soups, Salads & Sandwiches

Beer Cheese Soup

2 cloves garlic, minced
2 tablespoons Schmaltz or butter
4 cups rich chicken stock, fat removed
1/2 cup flour
1 can beer
1 pound grated sharp Cheddar cheese
1 teaspoon Lawrey's seasoned salt
1/2 teaspoon freshly ground black pepper
1/8 teaspoon cayenne pepper

In heavy saucepan, sauté garlic in Schmaltz or butter. Over medium heat, add chicken stock and bring to a boil. Stir in flour that has been whisked in beer. Cook until slightly thickened, stirring constantly. Add grated cheese and seasonings; stir constantly until cheese has melted. Serves 6.

Clubhouse Crab Bisque

10 1/2-ounce can condensed tomato soup
10 1/2-ounce can creamed pea soup
Two 10 1/2-ounce cans evaporated milk
7-ounce can crab meat
1 tablespoon sherry
1 pint whipped cream topping

Mix soups and milk in large double boiler and bring to boil. Drain crab meat and remove bones and add to soup. Just before serving pour in a tablespoon sherry. Warm soup tureen and soup plates in oven. When ready to serve pour hot soup in tureen and serve in individual soup plates, topped with whipped cream topping. Makes 6 servings.

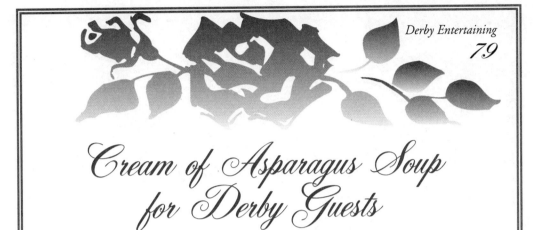

Cream of Asparagus Soup for Derby Guests

3 pounds asparagus
6 cups chicken broth
3 cups heavy cream
1/2 teaspoon salt
1/4 teaspoon pepper
2 1/2 tablespoons cornstarch
2 1/2 tablespoons water

Wash and trim asparagus. Cut into 1-inch pieces. Cook in salted water to cover until very soft and liquid is reduced by half. Strain and reserve cooking water. In blender, whirl asparagus and 2 cups of cooking liquid. May have to do in batches. Place mixture in a kettle with broth. Add cream, salt and pepper; bring to a slow boil. If a thicker soup is desired, mix cornstarch and water; whisk into soup. Makes 6 servings.

Kentucky Burgoo

1 stewing chicken
2 pound piece of beef chuck
1 1/2 pound lamb shoulder
1/2 veal shoulder
1 ham bone

Place all meats in a large pan, cover with water and season with salt and pepper. Cook until meat is tender and stringy. Cut and remove meat from bones. Return meat to broth and add:

1/2 bunch celery, chopped
1/2 pound carrots, chopped
1 1/2 pounds green beans, chopped
3 green peppers, chopped
3 medium onions, chopped
4 potatoes, chopped
1/2 head of cabbage, shredded
16-ounce bag frozen peas
16-ounce bag frozen sliced okra
16-ounce bag frozen corn

Three 15-ounce cans tomatoes
5 ounces Worcestershire sauce
10 ounces of catsup
1/4 cup vinegar

Cook until all vegetables are tender. Serve in mugs with fresh bread.

Cream of Leek Soup

5 to 6 medium leeks
6 tablespoons butter or margarine
3 tablespoons flour
2 teaspoons chopped chives
1/2 teaspoon salt
2 cups chicken broth
4 cups milk

Thinly slice leeks, removing green portion. Combine butter and leeks; cook over medium heat for 10 minutes, stirring occasionally. Stir in flour, chives and salt; cook 1 minute. Slowly add broth and milk. Cook over medium heat until mixture starts bubbling, stirring constantly. Serves 8.

Cold Cucumber Soup

8 cups chopped, peeled cucumbers
2 cups chopped green onions
1/2 cup margarine
1/2 cup flour
8 cups chicken broth
Salt and pepper to taste
1 cup evaporated milk
Cucumber slices for garnish

Cook cucumbers and onions over medium-high heat in margarine. Stir in flour. Gradually add broth, stirring until mixture thickens and begins to boil. Add salt and pepper. Cover; simmer over low heat for 10 minutes, stirring occasionally. Refrigerate until chilled. Mix some of the soup in blender until smooth. Strain blended mixture through sieve into a mixing bowl; discard seeds. Repeat with rest of mixture. Stir in evaporated milk. Pour into chilled serving bowls; garnish with cucumber slices. Serves 8 to 10.

Bibb Lettuce Salad

3 heads Bibb lettuce
1 medium red onion
1 can mandarin oranges, drained
Poppyseed dressing
1/3 cup toasted pecans

Wash lettuce leaves in cold water and dry. Thinly slice onion and separate into rings. Arrange lettuce leaves, onion rings and mandarin orange slices on a serving platter. Drizzle sparingly with Poppyseed Dressing and top with pecans. Makes 6 servings.

Poppyseed Dressing

1/3 cup honey
2 tablespoons vinegar
1 tablespoon frozen orange juice concentrate
1 tablespoon prepared mustard
1 teaspoon salt
3/4 cup canola oil
1 teaspoon poppy seeds

In a bowl combine honey, vinegar, orange juice concentrate, mustard and salt.
Gradually add oil whisking until well blended. Stir in poppy seeds. Makes 1
1/4 cups.

Dottie's Spinach Salad

Two 10-ounce packages fresh spinach, washed, drained and torn
Two 12-ounce cartons cottage cheese, rinsed
1 cup chopped pecans
1 cup sour cream
1/2 cup sugar
4 tablespoons vinegar
4 tablespoons horseradish
1 teaspoon dry mustard
1/2 teaspoon salt

Combine spinach, cottage cheese and pecans into large serving bowl. Mix together remaining ingredients for dressing; combine with spinach mixture. Serves 8.

Strawberry and Lettuce Salad

Leaf lettuce, green and red
Sliced strawberries

Dressing

3/4 cup sugar
1/2 cup red wine vinegar
1/4 cup olive oil
1 teaspoon paprika
1/2 teaspoon pepper
2 cloves garlic, minced

Mix lettuce and strawberries in large bowl. Mix dressing ingredients in microwave-safe bowl. Microwave on High for 1 minute to blend. May serve warm or cold over salad.

Wilted Lettuce Salad

8 heads Bibb lettuce
6 tablespoons bacon drippings
6 tablespoons sugar
Salt and pepper to taste
6 tablespoons vinegar

Wash and dry lettuce. Tear lettuce leaves into a salad bowl. Heat bacon drippings and add sugar, salt and pepper. Gradually add vinegar. Pour over lettuce and serve hot. Makes 8 servings.

California Chicken Salad

1/2 cup butter
2 cups mayonnaise
1/4 cup minced parsley
1/2 teaspoon curry powder
1/4 teaspoon minced garlic
Pinch of marjoram
Salt and pepper to taste
4 cups shredded cooked chicken breasts, about 4 small breasts
2 cups sliced, seedless green grapes
1/2 cup toasted, slivered almonds
Lettuce leaves

Melt butter in saucepan. Cool to room temperature. In a bowl, gently stir the butter into mayonnaise, parsley, curry powder, garlic, marjoram, salt and pepper. In a large bowl, combine chicken, grapes and almonds. Arrange this mixture on lettuce leaves. Spoon dressing on top and sprinkle with paprika. Serves 4.

Mother's Chicken or Turkey Salad

White chicken or turkey meat, cooked, cooled and cubed
Chopped celery
Toasted slivered almonds
Salt and pepper to taste
Mayonnaise
Slaw dressing

Mix chicken with celery, almonds, salt and pepper. Add enough mayonnaise to thoroughly moisten. Add just a small dollop of slaw dressing to give it a distinctive zip. Chill for up to 24 hours.

Derby Luncheon Chicken Salad

6 ounces lemon gelatin
2 cups boiling water
2 cups cream, whipped
8-ounce package cream cheese
1 1/2 cups chopped celery
1 cup sliced stuffed olives

Topping

3 to 4 cups diced chicken or turkey
1 pint mayonnaise
1 tablespoon chopped onion
1 1/2 tablespoons lemon juice

Dissolve lemon gelatin in boiling water; cool. When it reaches the consistency of egg whites, fold in whipped cream and cream cheese which has been softened with a little milk. Add celery and olives. Fold together gently and pour into a 9x12-inch pan that has been coated with mayonnaise. Chill. For topping, mix all ingredients together. Place squares of gelatin mixture on lettuce leaves. Spoon topping on individual servings. Garnish with tomato wedges, avocado slices or both. Serves 12 to 15.

Tropical Chicken Salad

3 cups chopped cooked chicken
2 mangoes, chopped
4 celery stalks, sliced
8-ounce can pineapple chunks, drained
1/2 cup toasted and chopped slivered almonds
1/2 cup Jalapeño-Lime Mayonnaise
1/2 teaspoon salt

Stir together first 5 ingredients in a medium bowl. Stir together mayonnaise and salt; stir into chicken mixture. Chill. Makes 6 servings.

Jalapeño-Lime Mayonnaise

1/2 cup mayonnaise
1 seeded and minced jalapeño pepper
1 teaspoon grated lime rind
2 teaspoons fresh lime juice

Stir together all ingredients; chill. Makes about 1/2 cup.

Chick Pea Salad

1 cup canned chick peas, rinsed and drained
1 cup 1/2-inch cubed cucumber
2 cups 1/2-inch cubed tomatoes
1 cup 1/2-inch cubed sweet yellow onion
2 tablespoons vinegar
1 tablespoon olive oil
2 tablespoons finely chopped basil
2 tablespoons finely chopped parsley
Salt and pepper to taste

In a large bowl combine the chick peas, cucumber, tomatoes, onion, basil and parsley. Add vinegar, olive oil and salt and pepper. toss to blend. Let stand 1 hour before serving Makes 6 servings.

Congealed Salad

1 can tomato soup
8-ounce package cream cheese
2 tablespoons unflavored gelatin
1/4 cup cold water
3/4 cup chopped pecans
1/2 cup chopped green peppers
1/4 cup chopped red onions
1/2 cup finely chopped celery
1 cup mayonnaise

Bring soup to a boil; add cream cheese and stir until smooth. Soften gelatin in cold water; add to soup mixture. Dissolve thoroughly and cool. Add nuts, pepper, onion, celery and mayonnaise. Mix well; pour into a mold and chill until firm. Unmold onto a serving plate of lettuce. Makes 8 servings.

Down to the Wire Pasta Salad

1 box large shell pasta
1 small sweet onion, diced
5 diced celery stalks
1 diced green pepper
1 diced red pepper
10-ounce package shredded Cheddar cheese
1 1/2 cups diced ham
2 1/2 cups mayonnaise
3 tablespoons Old Bay Seasoning
1/3 cup lemon juice
Salt and pepper to taste

Cook pasta per package directions; rinse and drain thoroughly; cool in refrigerator while preparing remaining ingredients. Blend together mayonnaise, Old Bay Seasoning and lemon juice until smooth; add all remaining ingredients. Stir thoroughly and chill overnight for best flavor. Serves 10.

Warm Baked Potato Salad

6 medium-size baking potatoes
1 small onion, chopped
2 hard-cooked eggs, chopped
2 celery stalks, chopped
1 cup mayonnaise
2 tablespoons spicy brown mustard
1 teaspoon garlic salt
1/2 teaspoon pepper
1/2 teaspoon dried dillweed
6 pimiento-stuffed olives, chopped
Fresh parsley for garnish

Bake potatoes at 400° for 1 hour or until tender; cool slightly. Remove top one-third of potatoes, cutting lengthwise; carefully scoop out pulp, leaving shells intact. Keep shells warm. Combine potato pulp, onions, egg, and celery in a medium bowl. Stir together mayonnaise and next 4 ingredients; stir into potato mixture. Spoon into potato shells. Sprinkle with olives, if desired. Garnish, with parsley. Serve immediately. Makes 6 servings.

Kentucky Spring Salad

2 eggs
1 teaspoon dry mustard
1 teaspoon salt
1/2 cup sugar
1 teaspoon flour
1/2 cup vinegar
1/2 cup cream
1 large head leaf lettuce
2 hard-cooked eggs, sliced
1/2 cup thinly sliced green onions

In the top of a double-boiler over hot water, beat eggs. Add mustard, salt, sugar, flour and vinegar. Cook, stirring, until mixture thickens. Add cream; cook until thickened. Cool and chill. Serve over lettuce, garnished with eggs and green onions. Makes 4 servings.

Overnight Vegetable Salad

1 1/2 cups vegetable oil
1/2 cup cider vinegar
3/4 cup confectioners' sugar
1 1/2 teaspoons grated orange rind
2/3 cup fresh orange juice
1 teaspoon salt
1 teaspoon Worcestershire sauce
3/4 teaspoon paprika
1/2 teaspoon dry mustard
2 garlic cloves, pressed
14 1/2-ounce can whole green beans, drained
15 1/4-ounce can sweet peas, drained
1/2 cup pimiento-stuffed olives, sliced
2 carrots, cut into thin strips
1 bunch celery, cut into thin strips
1 bunch green onions, sliced
2 green bell peppers, chopped
Cabbage bowl or cabbage leaves
2-ounce package slivered almonds, toasted

Stir together first 10 ingredients in a large bowl. Add green beans and next 6 ingredients. Cover and chill overnight. Drain and spoon into cabbage bowl. Sprinkle with toasted slivered almonds. Makes 12 servings.

Long Shot Seven-Layer Salad

1 head iceberg lettuce, chopped
1 cup chopped celery
1 cup chopped green peppers
1 1/2 cups chopped red onion
1 cup frozen peas, cooked
1 1/2 cups mayonnaise
2 tablespoons sugar
2 1/2 cups shredded Cheddar cheese
8 bacon slices, crisply cooked and crumbled

Arrange lettuce in the bottom of a deep clear bowl. In layers, add celery, green pepper, onions and peas. Do not toss. Spread mayonnaise evenly over peas. Sprinkle with sugar and cheese. Cover and chill for 4 hours. Sprinkle bacon over salad and toss when ready to serve. Makes 12 servings.

Baked
Chicken Salad Sandwiches

3 cups cooked and diced chicken breasts
2 hard-cooked eggs, peeled and chopped
1/4 cup chopped ripe olives
1/4 cup chopped celery
1/2 cup mayonnaise
1 tablespoon lemon juice
Salt to taste
12 slices white bread, crusts removed
1 can cream of chicken soup
1 cup sour cream
1 cup grated Cheddar cheese

Combine chicken, egg, olives, celery, mayonnaise, lemon juice and salt. Spread on bread slices to make 6 sandwiches. Place in a 13x9x2 inch baking dish. Combine soup and sour cream; spread over sandwiches. Cover and chill overnight. Uncover and bake at 325° for 20 minutes. Top with cheese and continue to bake until cheese melts. Serves 6.

Spicy Chicken Burgers with Creamy Horseradish

2 pounds ground chicken breast
1 cup chopped green onion
1/2 cup dry bread crumbs
4 teaspoons Worcestershire sauce
1/2 teaspoon salt
2 egg whites
8 hamburger buns, halved and lightly toasted
8 lettuce leaves

Combine chicken, green onion, bread crumbs, Worcestershire sauce, salt and egg white in bowl. Form eight patties, one-inch thick. Coat large nonstick skillet with nonstick cooking spray. Place over medium heat. Add patties, cover and cook until browned, about 5 minutes. Turn, cover and cook until no longer pink in center, about 5 minutes. To serve, spread each bun half with 1 tablespoon Creamy Horseradish, 1 patty and 1 lettuce leaf each. Top with remaining half of hamburger bun. Serves 8.

Creamy Horseradish

2 cups sour cream
1/2 cup drained bottled horseradish
1/2 teaspoon ground black pepper
4 tablespoons white-wine vinegar

Combine in a small bowl; refrigerate covered for up to 3 days.

Bar-B-Que Beefsteak Sandwich

Order 6 dozen tiny hamburger buns 2 or 2 1/2-inch in diameter
from your local bakery.
7 pounds round steak cut 2 1/2 to 3 inches thick
1/4 cup salt
1 lb. 2 oz. bottle prepared Bar-B-Q sauce

Rub salt into meat thoroughly. Place meat in a roaster with one quart of water. Cover and bake at 350° for 3 1/2 hours. Remove from pan reserving liquid. With 2 kitchen forks, on a wooden cutting board shred meat into small pieces, mix shredded meat with most of the juice leaving 1/2 cup to add to chafing dish during the evening to prevent meat from becoming dry. Add BBQ sauce and stir until well mixed. Serve hot from chafing dish on warm hamburger buns. Makes 36 servings.

Beef Tenderloin Sandwich

1/2 cup melted butter
1 tablespoon seasoned salt
2 tablespoons garlic powder
2 tablespoons cayenne pepper
One 5 pound beef tenderloin
Party rolls
Sour cream
Prepared horseradish

Combine butter, seasoned salt, garlic powder and cayenne pepper, mixing well. Place tenderloin on a rack in roasting pan. Brush with butter mixture and insert meat thermometer, not touching fat. Bake at 425° for 45 minutes or until thermometer reads 140° for rare, 150° for medium-rare or 160° for medium. Cool slightly and slice meat. Serve on party rolls with sour cream and horseradish. Makes 20 servings.

Cheese Steak Hoagies

2 tablespoons oil
1 medium onion, sliced
1 green pepper, cut into 1-inch pieces
1 pound thinly-sliced roast beef
8-ounce jar processed cheese spread
8 hoagie buns

Sauté onion and bell pepper over medium-high heat until tender. Push to one side of pan; add beef slices. Cook and stir until beef is heated. Slice hoagies in half; spread 2 tablespoons cheese on cut side of each hoagie bun. Arrange beef slices on bottom side. Top with onion and pepper mixture. May cut in half to serve. Makes 8 sandwiches/16 half sandwiches.

Classic Country Ham Salad

1 cup chopped cooked country ham
3/4 cup chopped sweet pickle
2/3 cup finely diced celery
1/4 cup finely grated onion
1/2 cup mayonnaise
1/2 teaspoon sugar

In a mixing bowl, combine ham, pickle, celery, onion and mayonnaise. Mix well. Sprinkle sugar evenly over mixture and blend well. Serve as sandwich filling or as a dip.

Kentucky Hot Brown

4 tablespoons butter
1/2 cup flour
4 cups milk
1/2 cup grated Cheddar cheese
1 1/2 cups grated Parmesan cheese, divided
1/2 teaspoon salt
1 teaspoon Worcestershire sauce
2 pounds cooked sliced turkey
16 slices toast, trimmed
8 slices tomato
16 slices bacon, cooked

Melt butter, add flour and stir well. Add milk, Cheddar cheese, 1/2 cup Parmesan cheese and seasonings. Cook, stirring constantly, until thick. Place turkey on toast and cover with cheese sauce. Top with tomato slices and bacon. Sprinkle with remaining Parmesan cheese. Bake at 425° until bubbly. Makes 8 servings.

Special Occasion Crab Cakes

1 pound crab meat, preferably back-fin
1/4 cup mayonnaise
2 tablespoons minced parsley
1/2 teaspoon salt
1/2 cup soft bread crumbs
2 beaten eggs
5 drops Tabasco sauce
Fine cracker crumbs
1 stick butter, margarine or oil
1 tablespoon horseradish

Combine all ingredients except crumbs, butter and horseradish. Mix together lightly. Form into desired size cakes but do not pack firmly. Pat lightly with cracker crumbs; chill for an hour so they are easier to handle. Heat butter in a large skillet and fry cakes until golden brown on all sides. Drain on paper towels and serve immediately on sandwich buns or as an entree.

Entrées

Chicken Noodle Bake

5 pound hen
5 small onions, chopped
2 green peppers, chopped
3 tablespoons butter
1 1/2 tablespoons flour
2 cups chicken broth
2 cups tomatoes, cut up
6-ounce can drained and pitted ripe olives, sliced
8-ounce can sliced mushrooms, drained
8-ounce package thin noodles
1 pound diced sharp Cheddar cheese
1 cup buttered bread crumbs

In a stock pot stew chicken in boiling water until tender. When cool enough to handle, remove skin and bones and cut meat into 1 1/2-inch pieces. Reserve 2 cups of chicken broth. Sauté onions and green peppers in butter until tender. Add flour; stir until smooth. Add broth and bring to a boil. Stir constantly until thickened. Add tomatoes, olives and mushrooms. Cook noodles according to package directions for al dente. Drain well. Layer half of noodles, chicken sauce and cheese in a 3-quart casserole. Repeat with a second layer. Top with bread crumbs and bake at 325° for 1 hour. Makes 10 servings.

Chicken Keene

1/3 cup butter
1/3 cup flour
1 cup chicken broth
1 1/2 cups cream
2 teaspoons salt
1/8 teaspoon pepper
Meat from 1 cooked hen, cubed
1 cup sliced mushrooms
1 pimiento, cut in strips
1 green pepper, cut in strips
Sherry to taste
Paprika
12 tart shells

Melt butter in top of double-boiler over hot water. Slowly stir in flour. Gradually add broth and then cream. Cook over medium heat until thickened, stirring constantly. Season with salt and pepper. Add chicken, mushrooms, pimiento, green pepper and sherry. Continue to cook until vegetables are softened. Spoon into prepared tart shells and sprinkle with paprika. Makes 12 servings.

Fast Track Chicken

8 boned chicken breasts
Salt and pepper to taste
2 cloves garlic, crushed
4 tablespoons olive oil
4 tablespoons tarragon vinegar
2/3 cup dry sherry

Sprinkle chicken with salt and pepper. Crush garlic into oil and vinegar in a skillet. Sauté chicken pieces until golden brown, turning frequently. Remove; place in a baking dish. Pour sherry over pieces and bake at 350° for 10 minutes. Serves 8.

Chicken Tetrazzini

2 pounds linguini pasta
Eight 10-ounce chicken breasts
4 cups seasoned flour
2 cups vegetable oil
6 cups heavy cream
3 cups grated Parmesan cheese
2 teaspoons thyme
2 teaspoons basil

Cook pasta according to directions on package. Slice chicken breasts into strips and dust with seasoned flour. Heat oil in sauté pan; add chicken and cook, without browning, until chicken is done. Remove excess oil in pan and add heavy cream, Parmesan cheese and herbs. Stir over medium flame until heated. When cheese is blended and sauce is thickened, add pasta. Toss together and serve immediately. Serves 8.

Creme De Volaille

3 cups ground cooked chicken
1/2 cup finely chopped fresh mushrooms
1 cup medium thick white sauce
1 small onion, minced
3 beaten eggs
1 cup cracker crumbs
1 teaspoon melted butter
2 teaspoons salt
1/3 teaspoon red pepper
1 chopped pimiento
4 parsley sprigs, chopped
Mushroom Cream Sauce

Combine chicken and mushrooms with white sauce. Add remaining ingredients and beat hard. Pack firmly into a well buttered mold. Place mold in a shallow pan filled with 1/2-inch water; steam in a 400° oven for 1 1/2 hours. Serve with mushroom cream sauce. Makes 8 servings.

Mushroom Cream Sauce

1 pound mushrooms, sliced
Butter
2 1/2 tablespoons flour
1 cup cream
1/2 cup milk
Salt to taste
Paprika to taste
Sherry to taste

Saute mushrooms in butter. Blend flour into cream and milk; add to mushrooms. Cook, stirring contantly, until smooth. Season with salt, paprika and sherry.

Baked Chicken Breasts with Spinach

4 packages chopped frozen spinach
3 whole chicken breasts, halved
Flour
Melted butter
Salt, pepper and granulated garlic
2 cartons whipping cream
Parmesan cheese
Paprika

Thaw and drain spinach. Pat spinach into buttered 9x13-inch casserole dish. Dip chicken breasts into flour and then butter. Place on top of spinach. Season well with salt, pepper and garlic. Pour whipping cream over top; sprinkle generously with Parmesan cheese and dust with paprika. Bake at 325° for 45 minutes to 1 hour. Serves 6.

Asparagus and Chicken in Patty Shells

Yolks of 2 hard-cooked eggs, sieved
1 tablespoon softened butter
1 cup cream
Salt and pepper to taste
2 cups diced cooked chicken breasts
1 cup cooked asparagus tips
6 baked patty shells

In skillet, combine egg yolks with butter to make a paste. Add cream and blend thoroughly. Season with salt and pepper; stir in chicken. Gently fold in asparagus. Warm over low heat and spoon into patty shells. Makes 6 servings.

Kentucky Derby Turkey Hash

6 tablespoons butter
1 1/2 cups chopped onion
1/3 cup chopped red pepper
2 cups fresh mushrooms, thinly sliced
1/4 cup all-purpose flour
1 tablespoon instant chicken bouillon granules
2 cups milk
1 tablespoon Worcestershire sauce
4 cups diced cooked turkey
1/4 cup finely chopped fresh parsley
Lacy Batty Cakes

Melt butter in large, heavy skillet. Sauté onion and pepper until tender, about 8 minutes. Stir in mushrooms. Sauté 2 minutes longer. Remove pan from heat. Stir in flour and instant bouillon. Gradually stir in milk and Worcestershire sauce. Return to heat. Bring to boil, stirring constantly. Boil and stir 1 minute. Stir in turkey and parsley. Heat through. Serve over Lacy Batty Cakes. Serves 6.

Lacy Batty Cakes

3/4 cup white cornmeal
1/2 teaspoon baking powder
1/2 teaspoon baking soda
1/2 teaspoon salt
1 cup buttermilk
1 slightly beaten egg
1/4 cup butter

Combine cornmeal, baking powder, baking soda and salt in a mixing bowl. In a small bowl, combine buttermilk and egg; stir into cornmeal mixture until cornmeal absorbs liquid. Preheat griddle to 400°. Lightly butter griddle. Bake 4 cakes at a time using 1 tablespoon batter for each cake. Bake until cakes begin to bubble and bottoms are golden, 2 to 3 minutes. Turn and bake 2 to 3 minutes longer. Makes 24 cakes.

Kentucky Country Ham

Many country hams are covered with mold when purchased. Scrub or cut off the mold, then rinse the ham with a mixture of equal parts of white vinegar and water. These hams always taste salty. To remove some of the saltiness and add moisture back into the ham, place it in a large kettle, cover with fresh water and soak overnight. Drain and cover again with fresh water. Bring water to a boil and cook 20 minutes per pound of meat. For best results insert a meat thermometer and cook to 165°. Remove skin, spread with 1 cup of brown sugar mixed with 2 tablespoons dry mustard. Decorate with pineapple slices and whole cloves. Brown in 375° oven for 15 minutes. Allow to cool before slicing. Wrap ham tightly in aluminum foil and refrigerate. Don't use plastic wrap as it holds too much moisture and speeds spoilage. Cooked country ham will keep in the refrigerator up to six weeks. One pound of cooked country ham will top 25 biscuits.

Lazy Way Country Ham

10 to 14 pound country ham
Cold water
1 tablespoon flour
1 turkey size Reynolds oven bag
4 cups water

To remove salt, soak ham completely covered in cold water for 24 hours. Drain. Shake flour in oven bag and place in a roasting pan at least 2 inches deep. Scrub ham in warm water with a stiff brush. Rinse well and place ham in bag. Add 4 cups water. Close bag with nylon tie and cut six 1/2 inch slits in top. Through a slit in bag, puncture thickest part of ham with a knife and insert meat thermometer into ham, not touching bone. Bake in preheated 325° oven until thermometer reads 160°, about 3 1/2 to 4 1/2 hours. Let stand in bag for 15 minutes. Trim skin and fat from ham. To serve, slice very thinly. Makes 20 to 28 servings.

Winner's Circle Country Ham

Six 4-ounce slices cooked country ham
2 tablespoons brown sugar
1/4 cup water

Place ham slices in a lightly greased 13x9x2-inch baking dish. Sprinkle with brown sugar. Pour water over ham. Cover with foil and bake at 350° for 30 minutes. Makes 6 servings.

Pork Tenderloin with Mustard Glaze

1/4 cup coarse mustard
2 teaspoons curry powder
2 cloves garlic, minced
1/4 teaspoon cinnamon
1 pork tenderloin, trimmed of fat

In small bowl, combine mustard, curry powder, garlic and cinnamon. Rub the mixture on the pork; refrigerate overnight. Insert a meat thermometer in thickest part of meat; place pork in oven-cooking bag and follow instructions for tying and slitting the bag. Roast pork at 350° to an internal temperature of 170°, 1 to 1 1/4 hours. Let stand 10 minutes before slicing. Serves 8.

Honey-Mustard Tenderloin

1/2 cup honey
2 tablespoons cider vinegar
2 tablespoons brown sugar
1 tablespoon prepared mustard
1 1/2 pounds pork tenderloin

Preheat oven to 400°. Line baking sheet with foil. In small bowl combine honey, vinegar, brown sugar and mustard. Brush pork with some of the sauce. Place on foil. Roast; baste with sauce after 15 minutes. Continue cooking until meat thermometer registers 160° when stuck in center. Will take 10 minutes or more. Slice and serve. Makes 6 servings.

Filet Mignon in Mustard Balsamic Vinegar Sauce

1 tablespoon olive oil
Six 1 1/2 inch thick beef tenderloin steaks
1/4 cup chicken broth
2 tablespoons balsamic vinegar
1 tablespoon Dijon mustard

Preheat oven to 425°. In ovenproof 12-inch skillet over medium-high heat in hot oil, cook filet mignon until browned on all sides, about 6 minutes. Place skillet in oven; bake about 5 minutes for rare or until desired doneness. Remove meat to warm platter; keep warm. To skillet add chicken broth, vinegar and mustard. Heat to boiling, stirring constantly and scraping until browned bits are dissolved and mixture reduces slightly. To serve, spoon sauce over steaks. Makes 6 servings.

Two Time Winner's Roast Tenderloin of Beef

1 beef tenderloin, trimmed
Butter
Salt and pepper to taste
1/3 cup beef consommé
2 tablespoons tomato puree
1/4 cup sherry

Begin with tenderloin at room temperature and rub with butter, salt and pepper. Roast the beef at 325° for 30 to 40 minutes. During roasting time, baste with two tablespoons melted butter 2 or 3 times. Remove tenderloin from pan. To the juices add the consommé, tomato puree and sherry. Let boil and pour over tenderloin. Serve thinly sliced, hot or cold. Serves 6 to 8.

Victory Shrimp Milano

1 pound peeled shrimp, cooked and drained
2 cups sliced mushrooms
1 cup green pepper, cut in strips
1 minced garlic clove
1/4 cup margarine
3/4 pound cubed Velveeta cheese
3/4 cup whipping cream
1/2 teaspoon dill weed
1/3 cup grated Parmesan cheese
8 ounces cooked and drained fettucini

In large skillet, sauté shrimp, vegetables and garlic in margarine. Reduce heat to low. Add Velveeta cheese, cream and dill. Stir until cheese is melted. Stir in Parmesan cheese; add fettucini. Toss lightly. Makes 6 servings.

Seafood Linguine

28-ounce can crushed tomatoes
1/2 cup dry white wine
1/2 cup chopped fresh parsley
2 tablespoons olive oil
3 garlic cloves, crushed
1 teaspoon salt
1/2 teaspoon dried basil
1/4 teaspoon freshly ground pepper
1/2 pound halibut or scrod, cut into chunks
6 ounces shrimp, shelled and deveined
6 ounces sea scallops, halved
1/2 cup halved pitted ripe olives
12 ounces linguine, cooked
1/3 cup grated Parmesan cheese
Parsley sprigs for garnish

In large saucepan, combine tomatoes, wine, parsley, oil, garlic, salt, basil and pepper. Bring to a boil over medium heat. Reduce heat to low; simmer, uncovered 20 minutes stirring occasionally. Add fish; cool 5 minutes. Add shrimp and scallops; cook 2 to 3 minutes or until shrimp turn pink and scallops are opaque. Stir in olives. Place linguine in large bowl. Spoon sauce over; sprinkle with Parmesan cheese. Garnish with parsley springs. Makes 6 servings

Stuffed Sole

1 cup chopped onion
Two 4 1/4-ounce cans rinsed and drained shrimp
4 1/2-ounce jar drained sliced mushrooms
2 tablespoons margarine
1/2 pound drained canned crabmeat
8 sole or flounder fillets
1/2 teaspoon salt
1/4 teaspoon pepper
1/4 teaspoon paprika
2 cans cream of mushroom soup
1/3 cup chicken broth
2 tablespoons water
2/3 cup shredded Cheddar cheese
2 tablespoons minced parsley
Cooked wild, brown or white rice or a mixture

Sauté onion, shrimp and mushrooms in margarine until onion is tender. Add crabmeat; heat through. Sprinkle fillets with salt, pepper and paprika. Spoon crabmeat mixture on fillets; roll up and fasten with a toothpick. Place in a greased 13x9-inch baking dish. Combine the soup, broth and water; blend until smooth. Pour over fillets. Sprinkle with cheese. Cover and bake at 400° for 30 minutes. Sprinkle with parsley; return to oven, uncovered for 5 minutes or until fish flakes easily with a fork. Serve over rice. Makes 8 servings.

Pasta with Shrimp and Artichoke Hearts

2 tablespoons olive oil
1 pound peeled and deveined large shrimp
2 teaspoons minced garlic
1/2 teaspoon pepper
1 1/2 cups chicken broth
1 cup mushrooms
2 jars rinsed and drained artichoke hearts
1 1/2 cups coarsely chopped plum tomatoes
1/2 cup chopped parsley
2 tablespoons butter
1/2 teaspoon each salt, dried oregano and basil
1 pound linguine, cooked

Heat oil in large skillet. Add shrimp and 1 teaspoon garlic. Cook over medium heat 3 to 5 minutes, stirring often, until shrimp turn opaque but are still translucent in center. Remove shrimp. Add remaining garlic, pepper and chicken broth to skillet. Bring to a boil; cook 3 to 5 minutes to reduce liquid slightly. Stir in artichoke hearts and tomatoes; cook 3 to 5 minutes. Add shrimp and cook about 2 minutes until mixture is hot and shrimp are no long translucent in center. Remove from heat. Stir in parsley, butter and seasonings. Pour over hot pasta and toss to mix. Makes 8 servings.

Grilled Orange Roughy Margarita

1 1/2 pounds orange roughy fillets
1/3 cup white or gold tequila
1/2 cup triple sec
3/4 cup fresh lime juice
1 teaspoon salt
2 large cloves garlic, crushed
1 tablespoon vegetable oil, divided
3 diced medium-size tomatoes
1 finely chopped medium white onion
1 tablespoon minced jalapeño or serano chilies
2 tablespoons chopped cilantro
Pinch of sugar
Freshly ground black pepper

Place fish in a glass dish large enough to hold fillets in a single layer. Combine tequila, triple sec, lime juice, salt, garlic and 2 teaspoons oil; pour over fish, rubbing all over. Cover and marinate for 1 hour at room temperature for 3 hours in the refrigerator, turning occasionally. Shortly before serving time, combine tomatoes, onions, chilies, cilantro, sugar and pepper to taste. Heat the grill to very hot. Remove fish from the marinade, reserving marinade. Pat

dry. Cook on greased grill for about 4 minutes per side or until fish flesh is opaque. Meanwhile boil marinade in saucepan for about 2 minutes; remove and discard garlic cloves. Spoon a little of marinade over fish. Spoon the tomato salsa alongside. Serves 6.

May also use red snapper, grouper or sea trout.

Vegetable Lasagna

8 lasagna noodles
10-ounce package frozen chopped broccoli
14 1/2-ounce can tomatoes
15-ounce can tomato sauce
1 cup chopped celery
1 cup chopped onion
1 cup chopped green or sweet red pepper
1 1/2 teaspoons dried basil
2 bay leaves
1 clove garlic, minced
2 beaten eggs
2 cups ricotta cheese or cottage cheese
1/4 cup grated Parmesan cheese
1 cup shredded mozzarella cheese

Cook noodles and broccoli separately according to their package directions; drain well. Set aside. Cut up canned tomatoes. In large saucepan stir together undrained tomatoes, tomato sauce, celery, onion, green pepper, basil, bay leaves and garlic. Bring to boiling; reduce heat. Simmer, uncovered, 20 to 25 minutes or until sauce is thick, stirring occasionally. Remove bay leaves. Meanwhile, in a bowl stir together eggs, ricotta cheese, Parmesan cheese and 1/4 teaspoon pepper. Stir in broccoli. Spread about 1/2 cup of the sauce in a

13x9x2-inch baking dish. Top with half of the noodles, half of the broccoli mixture and half of the remaining sauce. Repeat layers, ending with sauce. Bake, uncovered, in 350° oven for 25 minutes; sprinkle with mozzarella. Bake 5 minutes more or until heated through. Let stand 10 minutes before serving. Makes 8 servings.

Broccoli Lasagna

2 cans cream of broccoli soup
10-ounce package frozen chopped broccoli
4 tablespoons oil
3 thinly sliced carrots
1 large onion, diced
3/4 cup sliced mushrooms
8 lasagna noodles
16-ounce package shredded mozzarella cheese
15-ounce container cottage cheese
2 large eggs

Heat soup and frozen broccoli over medium-low heat until broccoli is thawed. In 10-inch skillet cook carrots and onion in 1 tablespoon of oil until lightly browned. Reduce heat to low; stir in 1/4 cup water. Cover and simmer 15 minutes or until vegetables are very tender. Remove to bowl. In same skillet over high heat, in 3 tablespoons oil, cook mushrooms until lightly browned and all liquid has evaporated. Stir in carrot mixture. Cook noodles according to package instructions. In bowl, mix mozzarella, cottage cheese and eggs. In 13x9-inch pan spread 1 cup broccoli sauce. Add half noodles, then half cheese, then all carrot mixture and half sauce. Repeat with noodles, cheese and ending with sauce. Bake 375° for 45 minutes. Let stand about 10 minutes before cutting. Serves 8.

Sides

Cheese Mushroom Casserole

1/2 cup chopped celery
1 1/2 pounds fresh mushrooms, sliced
1/2 cup chopped onions
3 tablespoons butter
2 cups milk
2 well beaten eggs
1 teaspoon salt
2 cups grated sharp Cheddar cheese
2 teaspoons dry mustard
1/2 teaspoon pepper
Seasoned bread crumbs

Sauté celery, mushrooms and onion in butter. In a saucepan, mix milk, eggs, salt, cheese, mustard and pepper. Alternate layers of vegetables and sauce in 2-quart casserole dish. Sprinkle with bread crumbs. Bake at 325° for 45 minutes. Makes 8 servings.

Asparagus Cheese Strata

6 slices stale white bread, crusts removed and cut into cubes
1 pound asparagus, cut into 1-inch pieces and cooked in boiling
water until crisp-tender
1 1/2 cups shredded Cheddar cheese
4 slightly beaten eggs
2 1/2 cups milk
2 tablespoons minced onions
1 1/2 teaspoons salt
1/8 teaspoon pepper
2 tablespoons butter

Arrange half of the bread in the bottom of a buttered 10x6x2-inch baking dish. Cover bread with the asparagus and sprinkle with cheese. Cover with remaining bread. Combine eggs, milk, onion, salt, pepper and butter. Pour over mixture in dish. Let stand for 20 minutes. Bake at 325° about 45 minutes until puffed and lightly browned. Serves 6.

Marinated Asparagus and Hearts of Palm

3 pounds asparagus, cleaned
Two 14-ounce cans hearts of palm, drained and cut into 1/2-inch pieces
1 cup canola oil
1/2 cup cider vinegar
3 garlic cloves, crushed
1 1/2 teaspoons salt
1 teaspoon pepper
Cherry tomatoes

Cook asparagus in boiling water until crisp-tender. Drain and cool in ice water; drain well. Combine asparagus and hearts of palm in a plastic container with a snap-top lid. In mixing bowl, whisk together oil, vinegar, garlic, salt and pepper. Pour dressing over vegetables. Put on lid and chill for 8 hours. Turn container occasionally. Serve with tomatoes. Serves 12.

Kentucky Lemon Asparagus

3 pounds asparagus, washed and trimmed to equal length
1 cup bread crumbs
1/2 cup butter
1 1/2 teaspoons grated lemon rind
Salt to taste

Cook asparagus in boiling water until crisp-tender. Drain and place on serving platter; keep warm. Brown bread crumbs in butter over medium heat. Add lemon rind and salt. Sprinkle over asparagus. Serves 12.

Lima Bean and Corn Casserole

1 cup dried lima beans
10-ounce package frozen corn, thawed
1 medium onion, chopped
1 can whole tomatoes
1/3 cup sour cream
3 slices bacon, slightly cooked and chopped
Salt and pepper to taste

Soak lima beans in cold water overnight. Drain and combine with corn, onion, tomatoes, sour cream, bacon, salt and pepper. Bake at 350° for 3 hours. Makes 8 servings.

Mother's Corn Pudding

2 1/2 cups whole kernel canned white shoepeg corn
2 large beaten eggs
1 teaspoon salt
1/8 teaspoon pepper
2 tablespoons melted butter
3/4 cup half and half
2 tablespoons sugar
1 to 2 shakes nutmeg

Drain corn well. Combine with beaten eggs and remaining ingredients. Bake in a greased baking dish at 350° for 35 to 45 minutes. When pudding has cooked about 15 minutes, stir it gently to prevent corn from settling to bottom. Cook until nicely browned on top and center is set. Note, no flour is used in this recipe so it will be light in texture. Makes 8 servings.

Baked Mushrooms

3 pounds mushrooms
Lemon juice
3 tablespoons minced onions
4 tablespoons butter
A-1 steak sauce to taste
2 tablespoons flour
4 tablespoons grated Parmesan cheese
1 cup milk
3 lightly beaten egg yolks
4 tablespoons Pepperidge Farm Herb Dressing, finely crushed
Butter

Clean, trim and dice mushrooms. Sprinkle with lemon juice. Simmer mushrooms with onion and butter for 2 minutes. Stir in steak sauce, flour and cheese; cook 2 minutes longer. Transfer to a buttered baking dish. Mix milk and egg yolks; pour over mushrooms. Sprinkle with dressing crumbs and dot with butter. Bake at 425° for 20 minutes until golden brown. Makes 8 servings.

Spanish Onion Pie

1/2 pound Spanish onions
2 bacon slices, cut into 1/2-inch pieces
1/4 cup diced green pepper
1/2 cup saltine cracker crumbs
2 tablespoons melted butter
1/2 teaspoon thyme
1 egg
1/2 cup milk
1/2 cup shredded Cheddar cheese

Cut onions into thin slices, about 1 1/2 cups. Cook bacon until crisp. Remove to paper towels to drain. Cook onion and pepper in bacon drippings until onion is transparent. Mix crumbs with butter and press into bottom of a loaf pan. Place onion mixture over crumbs. Sprinkle with bacon pieces and thyme. Beat egg and milk together; pour over onions. Top with cheese. Bake in preheated 350° for 25 minutes. Makes 8 servings.

Lucky Day Casserole

1/2 cup butter
1 onion, chopped
1/2 cup chopped celery
1/2 cup chopped green pepper
8-ounce can sliced water chestnuts, undrained
1 can mushroom soup
1/2 cup chopped pimiento
17-ounce can peas, drained

Melt butter over low heat; add onion, celery and green pepper. Cook until tender. Add water chestnuts, soup, pimiento and peas. Stir well and spoon into greased 2-quart casserole dish. Bake at 350° for 30 minutes. Makes 8 servings.

Baby Baked Potatoes with Bleu Cheese Topping

20 small new potatoes
1/4 cup canola oil
Kosher salt
1/2 cup sour cream
1/4 cup crumbled bleu cheese
2 tablespoons chopped fresh chives

Wash and dry potatoes. Pour oil into a bowl; add potatoes. Toss to coat well with oil. Dip each potato in salt to coat lightly. Spread potatoes on baking sheet. Bake in preheated 350° oven for 50 minutes until tender. In small bowl combine sour cream and bleu cheese. Cut a cross in top of each potato; press with fingers to open. Top each potato with a spoonful of cheese mixture; sprinkle with chives. Makes 20 servings.

Potato Trackside Casserole

6-ounce package hash browns mixed with onion
1 quart hot water
5 eggs
1/2 cup cottage cheese
1 cup shredded Swiss cheese
1 green onion, diced
1 teaspoon salt
1/2 teaspoon pepper
3 drops Tabasco sauce
6 bacon slices, cooked, drained and crumbled
Paprika

Cover hash browns with hot water in mixing bowl. Let stand for 10 minutes; drain well. Beat eggs and add potatoes, cottage cheese, Swiss cheese, green onion, salt, pepper and Tabasco sauce. Pour mixture into greased 10-inch pie pan. Sprinkle with bacon and paprika. Cover and chill overnight. Uncover and bake at 350° for 35 minutes. Makes 8 servings.

Long-Grain and Wild Rice Ring

2 tablespoons canola oil
1 large onion, chopped
2 cups processed long-grain and wild rice
5 cups chicken broth
1/2 cup dried currants
Salt to taste
6 green onions, cut diagonally in 1/4-inch pieces
Parsley sprigs

Heat oil and add onion; cook 5 minutes until softened. Add rice and stir to coat with oil. Add broth and bring to a boil. Reduce heat to low; stir currants into rice mixture. Add salt. Cover and simmer until rice is tender and all liquid has been absorbed, about 20 minutes. Transfer rice to a mixing bowl; stir in green onions. Spoon into an oiled 7-cup ring mold and gently pack down. Unmold onto a serving platter and fill center with parsley sprigs. Makes 8 servings.

Tomatoes Stuffed with Spinach

12 medium tomatoes
1 1/2 teaspoons salt
1 1/2 teaspoons sugar
Three 10-ounce packages frozen chopped spinach
1 medium onion, chopped
1/3 cup melted butter
3 tablespoons flour
1 1/2 cups milk
3/4 teaspoon salt
1/2 teaspoon white pepper

Cut top quarter off each tomato. Scoop out pulp, leaving shells intact. Sprinkle inside each shell with 1/8 teaspoon salt and 1/8 teaspoon sugar. Invert on paper towels to drain. Cook spinach according to package directions. Drain well by pressing out liquid with the back of a spoon. Sauté onion in butter until tender. Add flour, stirring to blend. Cook 1 minute, stirring constantly. Gradually add milk and cook over medium heat, stirring constantly, until mixture is bubbly and thickened. Stir in spinach, 3/4 teaspoon salt and pepper. Spoon spinach mixture into tomato shells. Place on a greased 13x9x2-inch baking dish. If desired, cover and chill for 24 hours. Let stand for 30 minutes and bake at 350° for 20 minutes. Makes 12 servings.

Vegetable Casserole

1 cup drained French style green beans
1 cup drained white shoepeg corn
1 cup cream of celery soup
8-ounce container sour cream
1/2 cup chopped celery
1/2 cup chopped green pepper
1/2 cup chopped onions
1 cup crushed Ritz crackers
1/2 stick butter, melted

Combine beans, corn, soup, sour cream, celery, green peppers and onions. Spoon into greased 1-quart casserole dish. Mix crackers and butter; spread over top of vegetable mixture. Bake at 350° for 45 minutes. Makes 8 servings.

Green Vegetable Casserole

1 small can pimientos, drained
1 can asparagus, drained
1 can peas, drained
1 small can sliced mushrooms, drained
3 tablespoons butter
3 tablespoons flour
1 1/2 cups milk
1/2 cup grated Cheddar cheese
1 cup crushed cheese Ritz crackers
Paprika

Dice pimientos and add to asparagus, peas and mushrooms. Melt butter, stir in flour and gradually add milk, stirring constantly until thickened. Add cheese and stir until cheese is melted. Place a layer of vegetables in bottom of a casserole dish; add a layer of cheese sauce. Repeat layers and top with cracker crumbs and paprika. Bake at 350° for 20 minutes. Makes 8 servings.

Escalloped Apples

2 cups bread crumbs
1/4 cup melted butter
1/4 cup brown sugar
Dash of salt
Few gratings of nutmeg
4 cups cooking apples, peeled, cored and diced
2 tablespoons lemon juice
1/2 cup hot apple juice

Combine bread crumbs with butter, brown sugar, salt and nutmeg. Place half of the crumb mixture in a shallow buttered baking dish. Add apples, then remaining crumbs. Mix lemon juice and apple juice together; pour over all. Bake at 350° until crumbs are brown and apples are tender. Time will depend on firmness of apples. Makes 6 servings.

Desserts

Apple Spice Cake

3 cups flour
2 cups sugar
1 1/2 teaspoons baking soda
1 teaspoon cinnamon
1 teaspoon allspice
1 teaspoon salt
2 eggs
1 cup canola oil
1 cup chopped walnuts
2 cups apples, cooked and pureed or one 16-ounce can apple pie filling
Confectioners' sugar
Bourbon sauce

In a mixing bowl combine flour, sugar, baking soda, cinnamon, allspice, salt, eggs, oil, walnuts and apples. Mix thoroughly and pour into a buttered 13x9x2-inch baking pan. Tap lightly on a flat surface to remove any air pockets. Bake in a preheated 300° oven for 50 minutes or until a cake tester comes out clean. Remove from oven and let cool in pan on a wire rack for 20 minutes. Turn out onto the rack and dust the top with confectioners' sugar. Serve with Bourbon Sauce. Serves 12.

Bourbon Sauce

1 cup brown sugar
2 tablespoons cornstarch
1/4 teaspoon salt
1 1/2 cups boiling water
4 tablespoons butter, cut into chunks
1 teaspoon vanilla extract
1/2 cup bourbon

Combine brown sugar, cornstarch and salt in saucepan; add the boiling water and cook over low heat for 5 minutes until thickened, stirring occasionally. Remove from heat and stir in butter, vanilla and bourbon. Serve warm over cake or ice cream.

Chess Cakes

1 pound light brown sugar
1 cup white sugar
4 eggs
1 cup butter
2 cups flour
3 teaspoons baking powder
1 teaspoon salt
1 teaspoon vanilla extract
1/2 cup pecans, chopped

Combine brown sugar, white sugar, eggs and butter. Beat until light. Sift together flour, baking powder and salt; blend into egg mixture. Mix well and add vanilla and nuts. Spoon into a greased and floured 13x9x2-inch baking pan. Bake at 325° for 45 minutes until firm around edges. Center will be soft. Since these are very rich, cut into 1-inch squares. Makes about 100 squares.

Quick Blackberry Jam Cake

One 1-pound 2-ounce spice cake mix
Eggs, oil and liquid as directed on package
1 cup blackberry jam

Combine cake mix according to package directions. Add jam and mix only until smooth. Pour into an ungreased 13x9x2-inch pan. Bake in a preheated 350° oven for time given on cake mix package or cake tests done. Cool in pan on a wire rack. Frost with caramel icing.

Caramel Icing

1/4 pound butter
1/3 cup half and half
1 1/2 cups brown sugar
1 1/2 cups confectioners' sugar
1 teaspoon vanilla extract

Heat butter, half and half and brown sugar until butter is melted and sugar dissolved. Beat in confectioners' sugar and vanilla. Spread on cake.

Kentucky Bourbon Balls

3 cups vanilla wafers
1 cup pecans
1 cup confectioners' sugar
3 tablespoons light corn syrup
1 1/2 tablespoons cocoa
1/2 cup bourbon
Extra confectioners' sugar for rolling

Grind wafers and nuts finely in food processor. Mix thoroughly with remaining ingredients; chill. Roll into balls the size of large cherries. Roll in confectioner's sugar. Makes about 35 balls.

Kentucky Chocolate Bourbon Balls

1/2 cup softened butter
16-ounce package confectioners' sugar
1/4 cup bourbon
1 cup chopped pecans
Four 1-ounce squares semi-sweet chocolate
Four 1-ounce squares unsweetened chocolate
Pecan halves

Cream butter and gradually add sugar, beating well at medium speed. Add bourbon; beat until smooth. Stir in chopped pecans. Chill and shape into 1-inch balls. Cover and chill for 8 hours. In a double-boiler over boiling water, combine all squares of chocolate. Reduce heat to low and cook, stirring often, until chocolate melts. Using a toothpick, pierce each ball and dip in chocolate. Place on waxed paper. Gently press a pecan half on top of each ball. Chill until chocolate hardens. Makes about 48 candies.

Bourbon Dates

Pitted dates
Bourbon
Pecan halves
Granulated sugar

Soak dates in bourbon overnight. Drain and put pecan in center of each date.
Roll in sugar. Store in an airtight container.

Mint Julep Kisses

2 egg whites
3/4 cup sugar
2 drops green food coloring
1 teaspoon peppermint extract
6 ounces chocolate bits

Beat egg whites until stiff, gradually adding sugar. Beat in food coloring and peppermint extract. Stir in chocolate bits and drop by spoonfuls onto a baking sheet. Put in an oven preheated to 325°. Immediately turn off heat. Leave in oven for several hours or overnight. Store in an airtight container. Makes 24.

Derby Brownies

1/2 cup softened butter
1 cup sugar
4 eggs
1 cup flour
1/4 teaspoon salt
16-ounce can chocolate syrup
1 cup chopped pecans
1/2 teaspoon almond extract
1/4 cup softened butter
2 cups sifted confectioners' sugar
2 1/2 tablespoons green creme de menthe

In a mixing bowl cream 1/2 cup of butter. Beating on medium speed gradually add sugar. Add eggs one at a time, beating after each addition. In another bowl combine flour and salt. Add to butter mixture alternately with chocolate syrup, beginning and ending with flour mixture. Stir in pecans and almond extract. Spoon into greased and floured 13x9x2-inch baking pan. Bake at 350° for 25 minutes until a tester in center comes out clean. Cool in pan. Combine 1/4 cup butter, confectioners' sugar and creme de menthe. Beat at medium speed of mixer until smooth. Spread over top of brownie layer. Cool and chill for 1 hour. Cut into 1 1/2-inch squares. Makes 48 brownies.

Winning Ticket Lemon Bars

2 sticks butter
2 cups flour
1/2 cup confectioners' sugar
4 beaten eggs
2 cups sugar
4 tablespoons flour
4 tablespoons lemon juice
Confectioners' sugar

Blend butter, 2 cups flour and confectioners' sugar. Pat into a 13x9x2-inch pan. Bake in a preheated 325° oven for 20 minutes. To prepare second layer, blend together eggs, sugar, 4 tablespoons flour and lemon juice. Pour over first layer. Return to oven and bake at 325° for 20 minutes. Loosen around edges, cut into bars and sift confectioners' sugar over the top while warm.

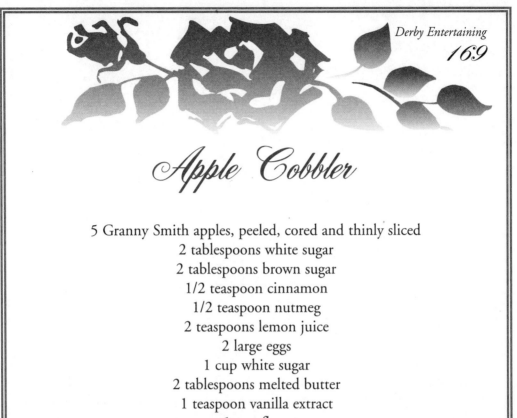

Apple Cobbler

5 Granny Smith apples, peeled, cored and thinly sliced
2 tablespoons white sugar
2 tablespoons brown sugar
1/2 teaspoon cinnamon
1/2 teaspoon nutmeg
2 teaspoons lemon juice
2 large eggs
1 cup white sugar
2 tablespoons melted butter
1 teaspoon vanilla extract
1 cup flour
1 teaspoon baking powder
1/2 teaspoon salt

In a large mixing bowl combine apples, white sugar, brown sugar, cinnamon, nutmeg and lemon juice. Mix well and pour into an oiled 8x8x2-inch baking pan. In a medium bowl beat eggs and white sugar on medium speed until blended. Add butter and vanilla; mix until smooth. In another bowl combine flour, baking powder and salt. Fold into egg mixture and spread over apples. Bake at 350° for 30 minutes until lightly browned. Makes 6 servings.

Kentucky Blackberry Cobbler

2 quarts fresh blackberries
4 tablespoons melted butter
2 cups flour
2 cups sugar
4 teaspoons baking powder
1/2 teaspoon salt
2 cups milk

Wash and remove stems from berries; drain thoroughly. Pour the melted butter into a 2-quart rectangular dish. Beat together flour, sugar, baking powder, salt and milk. Pour into buttered dish. Arrange berries evenly over batter. Bake in a preheated 400° oven for 35 minutes until crust is golden brown. If desired, serve with whipped cream or vanilla ice cream. Makes 10 servings.

Peach Cobbler

11 cups peeled, sliced peaches, about 5 1/2 pounds fresh
or 4 1/2 pounds frozen
3 tablespoons lemon juice
1/2 cup sugar
3 tablespoons flour
3 tablespoons butter, cut into pieces
2 cups flour
1/3 cup sugar
1 tablespoon plus 1 teaspoon baking powder
1/2 teaspoon salt
1/2 cup butter
1/2 cup cream
2 large eggs
2 teaspoons grated lemon peel

Combine peaches with lemon juice and 1/2 cup sugar; mix in 3 tablespoons flour. Pour peaches into a 13x9x2-inch pan and dot with 3 tablespoons butter. Place in a preheated 400° oven for 5 minutes while preparing batter. Sift together 2 cups flour, 1/3 cup sugar, baking powder and salt. Cut in 1/2 cup butter until mixture resembles coarse cornmeal. Stir in cream, eggs and lemon peel. Drop 14 mounds of batter over heated peaches and spread each mound slightly. Bake 25 minutes until dough is golden brown. Makes 14 servings.

Bourbon Apple Pie

1/2 cup raisins
4 tablespoons bourbon
7 cups peeled, cored and sliced apples
1 cup sugar
2 tablespoons flour
1 teaspoon cinnamon
1/8 teaspoon nutmeg
1/2 cup chopped walnuts
9-inch unbaked pie shell

Soak raisins in 2 tablespoons bourbon. Sprinkle remaining bourbon over apples. Combine sugar, flour, cinnamon and nutmeg. Add sugar mixture, raisins and nuts to apples; mix well. Spoon into pie shell. Bake in lower third of preheated 425° oven for 1 hour. Serves 6.

After-the-Race Caramel Pie

18 candy caramels
1/3 cup milk
1/2 cup sugar
1/4 cup water
1 tablespoon lemon juice
1 teaspoon vanilla extract
1 unbeaten egg white
1 cup heavy cream
9-inch baked pie shell
1 jar caramel ice cream topping
3/4 cup chopped pecans

In top of a double boiler, melt caramels with milk. Remove from heat and stir in sugar, water, lemon juice, vanilla and egg white. Set aside. Whip cream until thick. Gently fold into caramel mixture. Spoon half of mixture into pie shell. Pour half of caramel topping over top. Add remaining filling, then rest of caramel topping. Stir with the tip of a small knife blade to swirl caramel sauce through pie. Sprinkle with nuts. Serves 6.

Buttermilk Chess Pie

2 tablespoons flour
1 cup sugar
2/3 cup buttermilk
4 beaten eggs
1 stick butter, melted
Pinch of salt
1 teaspoon vanilla extract
1 unbaked 9-inch pie shell

In a mixing bowl mix flour and sugar. Combine with buttermilk, eggs, butter, salt and vanilla, mixing by hand. Pour into pie shell and bake at 325° for 45 minutes until set. Makes 1 pie, about 6 servings.

Shaker Lemon Pie

2 large lemons
2 cups sugar
4 well beaten eggs
1 unbaked 9-inch pie shell

Slice lemons paper thin, rind and all. Combine with sugar and mix well. Let stand for 2 hours, stirring occasionally. Add eggs to lemon mixture, blending well. Spoon into pie shell, arranging lemon slices evenly. Bake at 450° for 15 minutes. Reduce heat to 375° and bake 20 minutes longer; cool. Serves 6.

Southern Pecan Pie

3 eggs
2/3 cup sugar
Dash of salt
1 cup dark corn syrup
1/3 cup melted butter
1 cup pecan halves
1 unbaked 9-inch pie shell

Beat eggs with sugar, salt, corn syrup and butter. Add pecans and pour into pie shell. Bake at 350° for 50 minutes until a toothpick inserted between outside and center comes out clean. Cool. Serves 6.

Run For The Roses Pie

1 cup sugar
1/2 cup flour
1/2 cup melted butter
2 slightly beaten eggs
3/4 cup chopped pecans
6 ounces semi-sweet chocolate chips
1 teaspoon vanilla extract
2 tablespoons bourbon
1 unbaked 9-inch pie shell

Combine sugar and flour in a mixing bowl; mix in butter. Add eggs, nuts, chocolate chips, vanilla and bourbon; mix well. Pour into pie shell. Place on a baking sheet and bake in preheated 325° oven for 55 minutes until top is golden brown. Serves 8.

Old Talbott Tavern Pie

3/4 cup sugar
1/2 cup flour
1/4 teaspoon salt
1 1/4 cups water
2 beaten egg yolks
1/2 cup orange juice
1 tablespoon grated orange rind
2 tablespoons lemon juice
1 baked 9-inch pie shell
Whipped cream

In top of double-boiler over hot water combine sugar, flour and salt. Add water and stir until smooth. Cook, stirring constantly, over direct heat for 5 minutes. Remove from heat, add egg yolks stirring constantly; cook for 5 minutes longer over boiling water. Remove from heat. Add orange juice, orange rind and lemon juice. Chill and spoon into pie shell. Top with whipped cream. Serves 8.

Bourbon Peaches

4 peeled peach halves
4 tablespoons brown sugar
2 tablespoons butter
4 tablespoons bourbon

Places peaches in an 8x8x2-inch baking dish. Put equal parts of brown sugar, butter and bourbon in each peach cavity. Bake at 325° until sauce is hot and bubbly. Makes 4 servings.

Chocolate Bourbon Tarts

1/2 cup softened butter
1 cup sugar
2 eggs
1/2 cup flour
Pinch of salt
2 tablespoons bourbon
1 cup semi-sweet chocolate chips
1 cup chopped pecans
Small tart shells

Cream butter and sugar; add eggs and mix well. Add flour, salt and bourbon, stirring to blend. Mix in chocolate chips and nuts. Spoon into tart shells; fill 3/4 full. Bake at 350° for 25 minutes until lightly browned. Makes 50.

Bite-Size Tart Shells

1 cup flour
1 stick butter, softened
3-ounce package cream cheese
1/4 teaspoon salt

Combine all ingredients; mix well. Chill thoroughly. Place small ball of dough in each tart shell cup. Pat in bottom and up sides. Prick bottoms with a fork. Bake at 350° for 10 minutes until golden brown. Allow to cool in cups. Remove from cups and freeze, if desired, in an airtight container. Makes about 60 small size tart shells.

Blackberry Sherbet

1 pint fresh blackberries, washed and picked over
1/2 cup honey
1/2 cup evaporated milk
2 tablespoons lemon juice

Process all ingredients in a blender until smooth. Pour into an ice cream freezer and freeze according to manufacturer's directions. Makes 2 pints.

Strawberries Dipped In White Chocolate

2 pints strawberries
6 ounces white chocolate

Rinse strawberries, leaving stems attached. Dry carefully and thoroughly on paper towels since chocolate will not stick to wet berries. Set aside. Melt chocolate in top of a double-boiler over boiling water. Grasp strawberries by the stems; dip into melted chocolate and place on a wire rack sprayed with vegetable oil. Chill until firm. Serve within 8 hours. Makes 36 to 48.

Bread Pudding With Bourbon Sauce

3/4 cup brown sugar
2 tablespoons butter
4 slices bread
1 cup raisins
3 eggs
2 cups milk
1 teaspoon vanilla extract
1/8 teaspoon salt

For sauce

1/2 cup butter
1 cup sugar
3 tablespoons water
1 beaten egg
Bourbon to taste

In top of double-boiler over hot water add brown sugar. Butter bread slices, dice into cubes and sprinkle over sugar. Add raisins. Beat eggs with milk; stir in vanilla and salt. Pour over bread but do not stir. Cook over simmering

water for 1 hour. To make sauce, combine butter, sugar and water in a saucepan. heat until sugar dissolves. Beat together egg and sugar mixture, adding small amounts of mixture at a time. Return egg mixture to hot saucepan, stirring constantly. Add bourbon and serve over warm bread pudding. Serves 4.

Bourbon Date Pudding

2 eggs
1 cup sugar
5 tablespoons light cream
3 tablespoons flour
1 1/2 teaspoons baking powder
1 cup broken walnuts or pecans
1 cup chopped dates
2 tablespoons bourbon
Sweetened whipped cream

Combine eggs and sugar; beat until light and creamy. Add cream, flour, baking powder, nuts and dates into top of a double-boiler. Cover and cook over boiling water. Cook 2 hours, stirring occasionally, adding water to bottom of double boiler if necessary. When cooked, add bourbon and chill. Serve cold with sweetened whipped cream. Serves 8.

Woodford Pudding

1/2 cup softened butter
1 cup sugar
3 slightly beaten eggs
1 teaspoon baking soda
1/2 cup buttermilk
1 cup flour
1 teaspoon ground cinnamon
1 cup blackberry jam

Cream butter and sugar until light. Add eggs, one at a time, beating after each addition. Dissolve baking soda in buttermilk and set aside. Sift together flour and cinnamon. Add buttermilk and flour mixture to creamed mixture, alternately, beating well after each addition. Stir in jam and pour into a greased 12x7 1/2x2-inch baking pan. Bake at 350° for 40 minutes. Cool for 10 minutes in pan and turn out. Makes 15 servings.

Apple Pinoche

4 to 5 cooking apples, peeled, cored and sliced
Lemon juice
1/2 cup sugar
Butter
3/4 cup whipping cream

Topping

8 ounces cream cheese
1/4 cup whipping cream

Dip sliced apples in lemon juice. Arrange apples in overlapping circles in a well-buttered oven proof dish or quiche pan. Sprinkle with sugar and dot with butter. Bake at 350° for 45 minutes. Increase temperature to 400° and bake 15 minutes. Serve with topping.

For topping: Blend all ingredients and serve over apples.

Index

Food Source Guide

A Taste of Kentucky
Village Square Shopping Center
11800 Shelbyville
Louisville, KY 40243
(502) 244-3355
(502) 244-7014 Fax
1-800-444-0552
Website: www.atasteofkentucky.com

Mall of St. Matthew's
5000 Shelbyville
Louisville, KY 40207
(502)895-2733
1-800-444-0552
(502)244-7014 Fax
Specialty: Derby party supplies.

Applecreek Orchards
P. O. Box 8383
Lexington, KY 405333
(800) 747-8871
www.applecreek.net
Specialty: The finest preserves, butters, unique cakes in a jar, marinades, relishes and chocolate fudge sauces, some made with bourbon.

Boulevard Distillers & Importers, Inc.
P. O. Box 180
Lawrenceburg, KY 40342
Specialty: Wild Turkey Bourbon 101 Proof Rare Breed and Kentucky Spirit. Their products can be ordered anywhere by calling (800)BE-THERE. They have recipe cards.

Broadbent's
B&B Food Products, Inc.
5695 Hopkinsville Road
Cadiz, KY 42211-9987
(270)522-6674 KY Residents
(800)841-2202 Out-of State
(270)235-5182 Fax
Specialty: Country ham cured with honey, sugar and salt for 9 to 12 months. Seven-time winner of the Kentucky State Fair Grand Champion County Ham Award. They also sell sausages, country bacon, smoked turkey and gourmet food packs. Call for their mail order catalog.

Dolfinger's
The Forum Center
154 N. Hurstbourne Parkway
Louisville, KY 40222
(502)412-3634 or (502)412-0411
(502)412-0443 Fax
1-800-561-1314
Website: Louisville.com (under Dolfinger's)
Specialty: Although this is a fine jewelry and accessory store, they also sell classic silver mint julep cups. Write or call them for prices.

Gethsemani Farms, Inc.
Box KGC
3642 Monks Road
Trappist, KY 40051
(502)549-3117
1-800-549-0912
Website: www.monks.org
Specialty: A wonderful Trappist cheese that is served at the White House! The monks suggest crumbling their fruitcake and adding it to butterscotch or vanilla pudding. They have world-wide mail order service.

Hodgeson Mill, Inc.
P. O. Box 430
Teutopolis, IL 62467
(217)347-0105
(800)500-0202
Specialty: Kentucky Colonel Seasoned Flour, an excellent product. They have two recipe folders and a mail order price list for all their products.

Jackson Biscuit Company
John and Judy Jackson
725 Terry Drive
Winchester, KY 40391
(606) 745-2561
Website: www.jacksonbiscuit.com
Specialty: Beaten biscuits. Recognized by the state as the true "Kentucky food product" they make and sell beaten biscuits by mail order and at many central Kentucky groceries. A family business, everything is done by hand, using an old-fashioned biscuit machine and one special biscuit cutter.

Maker's Mark Distillery, Inc.
3350 Burks Spring Road
Loretto, KY 40037
(270)865-2881
Website: maker'smark.com
Specialty: Maker's Mark Bourbon. Maker's Mark VIP (personalized bottle) and Maker's Mark Mint Julep which is available in spring. Not sold by catalog.

Mom Blakeman's Candy, Inc.
209 Lexington Street
Lancaster, KY 40444
(606)792-3464
(800)542-4607
Specialty: Cream pull candy. They sell it plain, chocolate